Love God
Get Divorced

♥ | ⌾

Love God Get Divorced

LIVING LIFE WITH NO CONDITIONS

MIKE MOORE

Copyright 2022 © by Mike Moore

ALL RIGHTS RESERVED. No part of this book may be used or reproduced in any manner without written permission of the author or publisher.

For more information contact:
www.mikemooreonline.com

Printed in the United States of America.

Library of Congress Control Number: 20229-01803

ISBN: 978-1-956065-02-2

Unless otherwise noted, Scripture quotations are from the ESV® Bible (The Holy Bible, English Standard Version®), Copyright © 2001 by Crossway, a publishing ministry of Good News Publishers. Used by permission. All rights reserved.

Scripture quotations from the King James Version are noted with KJV.

Scripture taken from the New King James Version®. Copyright © 1982 by Thomas Nelson. Used by permission. All rights reserved. Noted with NKJV.

Published by EDK Books & Distribution, LLC
www.edkbooksanddistribution.com

Cover design by Julie K. Lee/Lee Creative
jkleecreative@gmail.com

Contents

FOREWORD	VII
ACKNOWLEDGEMENTS	XI
INTRODUCTION	XIII

PART I / THE BLANK CANVAS — 1
1. From My Heart — 3
2. Divorcing the Law — 12
3. Make the Past Not Last — 19
4. Fear Sucks — 25
5. Killing the Need for Greed — 32
6. Who Died and Made You Judge? — 39
7. My Pride Is Better Than Your Pride — 47

PART II / BEGINNING TO SKETCH — 51
8. Think You're Having a Bad Day? — 53
9. Extracting the Precious from the Vile — 63
10. Satan's Sperm — 71
11. The Death Zone — 83
12. Paul Is Not the New Moses — 86
13. Counterfeit Christianity — 97
14. The Love of a Prince — 104
15. Manasseh Meme — 112

PART III / ADDING THE PAINT — 119
   16. What's Essential? — 121
   17. #TheCrossMatters — 128
   18. Cancel Culture Began in the Church — 144
   19. Dead Man Walking — 155
   20. Wanna Be a Leader? Lead! — 162
   21. Apostle 13 — 166

PART IV / THE FINAL MASTERPIECE — 183
   22. Real Love Is in Forgiving — 185
   23. Along Comes Mary — 201
   24. Fourteenth Generation — 210
   25. Don't Have a Prayer? — 221
   26. Better Rich Than Bitch — 229
   27. Confessions of a Seat Saver — 241
   28. Where's Waldo? — 247
   29. Can I Divorce My Spouse? — 254

FOREWORD BY MICHAEL MILLER

SPOILER ALERT: this book is NOT about your marriage. This book has but one chapter to do with marriage. Yet this book has the potential to change not only your marriage but also your life. *Love God Get Divorced* is about your relationship with God.

One of the greatest lessons I've learned from Mike Moore is how NOT to relate to God. I have had the privilege of walking alongside Mike for nearly a decade. I've spent hours in his living room, studying scriptures, praying, discipling men, and enjoying Jesus together. His passion in life is to see people set free from religion and experience the unconditional love of God.

His passion is to connect the disconnected, burned out, disfranchised, and religiously worn-out people back to the Person of Christ. Religion robs us from receiving everything that Jesus has already provided for us.

For most of my Christian life, my relationship with God was based on performance. I lived under an internal

scoreboard for good and bad living, right and wrong doing. As Mike says, I had my "LIST," my measurements:
"Did I have bad thoughts today?"
"Look at the wrong stuff?"
"Cuss?"
"Chew?"
"Have I prayed today?"
"Read God's Word?"
"Shared the Gospel?"
It was ALL about metrics for me.

Over time, I felt like I was a complete loser at life, a guy who constantly disappointed God. The part of God I related to the most was His index finger. I figured it was usually extended and pointing directly at me! I was not pleased with myself and felt that He, for sure, was not pleased with me. The harder I tried, the worse it seemed to get.

You see, I grew up around God. I went to church weekly, Sunday school, a Christian college, and was even a pastor for several years—all the while burdened with a twisted view of God. What I did not realize is that religion had married me to a metric system.

Religion was the only means I had to God. Religion provided me a list of things I needed to do to be in right standing with God. This list was ever growing and ever changing, but the one constant was this: I could never meet what that list demanded.

The biblical word for this list is "the Law." It's what measures the problem that all of us who are walking the earth are trying to cure: sin. Yet religion is terrible because it demands something that can never be achieved. It only points out the problem without supplying any solutions.

I pray this book will help you find the only solution to this problem: JESUS. Mike masterfully dissects the ways we have been married to wrong thinking in our lives, our relationships, and our views of God. Each chapter deals with a major obstacle in our lives that hinders us from receiving and walking in God's grace.

We have heard that God loves us. We have heard that He forgives us. Yet wrong thinking and wrong beliefs about God will rob us of truly being able to LIVE in that reality.

The *Get Divorced* part of the title is actually a take on Paul's words in Romans 7. One must DIE to the law in order to be married to grace (Christ). It is only through death that we will find true freedom to lay down our false metrics and measurements to achieve something He has already (totally) provided.

We are challenged by this book to divorce ourselves from unforgiveness, greed, lust, fear, pride, and alignments we have made (via wrong thoughts) about ourselves and God. Through death in Christ, we DIED to the LAW (lists, metrics, and scoreboards) to be MARRIED to Christ. Praise God!

I'm indebted to Mike Moore. He has embodied the teachings in this book to me, and I'm excited for YOU to be transformed by the renewing of your mind into these Truths.

Michael Miller, Senior Pastor
Upper Room, Dallas, TX
www.urdallas.com

ACKNOWLEDGEMENTS

I want to thank my manifold group of friends for standing by me for these three books! My titles offend the religious—which I enjoy. The goal is to push, challenge, and excite people to engage with God's unconditional love!

To name whom to thank would take as many words as are in this book! Over fifty thousand! At a minimum, we're talking about my parents, my brother, my nephews and nieces, my friends, my scribes, and strangers that God has used to shape me into who I am today!

That said, whenever I don't like the way God expresses Himself through a particular individual or group, it's God I'm having an issue with, NOT them.

Introduction

Why this book? Because people are hanging on to false ideas and impressions of who God is and how He relates to us. That causes unnecessary stress, feelings of abandonment, loneliness, and depression.

This book is written for people who are tired of the BS of institutional church experiences that are so structured that the Holy Spirit can't even enter the room and who feel they have targets on their back when around unloving, *religious people*.

We've reduced Christianity to a man standing up front behind a box telling us what we should know and do because we (evidently) can't read the Scriptures for ourselves. The Gen X to Gen Z youth are bored with it, Millennials see little or no value in it, and many of the baby boomers don't even want to be there, but their spouses made them come. *Can you blame them?* The dynamic individualistic elements of the first-century Body of Christ has been replaced by shallow, corporate, entertainment, and prosperity teachings that do little to save the soul that hungers and thirsts for the goodness and holiness of God. So, like the unwanted emails that show up in your inbox, you decided *to unsubscribe* from God's messages by not going to a church that is better at claiming to know Jesus than acting like Him. *I get that.*

This book is also written for the person sitting on a street corner with a needle up his arm because he believes God has given up on him and the prostitute who is using sex to make enough money each week to feed her kids and get them a decent education.

In a word, all the people I've described are disenfranchised. As a meme on my Instagram page says: "If being hurt by the church causes you to lose faith in God, then your faith was in people, not God."

The typical Western church has become like an *ecclesiastical franchise operation*, and the parent company is the denomination that oversees it. Like other corporate franchises, there are standards to be kept and money that flows into the franchiser.

Gone is just about everything Jesus said in His Sermon on the Mount that would engage all age groups and give them a much deeper passion for God and His Word, that would heal the brokenhearted, and that would let the drug addict and the prostitute know they have a Friend that will stick closer than a brother and a heavenly Father that has been pursuing an eternal relationship with them since their births.

In institutional (franchise) churches, there are always winners and losers. Without question, the got-it-together ones always look down on the others (mostly behind their backs). That is not how God ever designed it to be. We are all losers, all guilty, all bankrupt of anything to justify ourselves before a holy and sovereign Judge. But God sent His Son to be the "biggest loser" of pride, position, and wealth so we could be winners in the Lamb's Book of Life and be flooded with the supernatural intensity of God's love, joy, peace, and security. When we walk into a church expecting that flood of godliness to cleanse us and satisfy our soul, we are confronted with the fact that someone has diverted that holy flood and replaced it with counterfeit love, counterfeit joy, counterfeit peace, and zero security.

By nature, that leads us from faith *in God* to faith *in our faith* (our denomination or creed). Many churches' missions are simply to perpetuate themselves and maybe replicate their franchises in other places (also known as "church planting"). Those aren't the mission statement words on the wall, but that's how it plays out. It has ceased to righteously proclaim Christ to a dying world . . . and a dying church for that matter. Being disenfranchised from a pseudo-religious culture is a good thing *whether we choose* to do it or whether it is thrust upon us.

In reading this book, there may be times where it's going to feel like "OMG we're sinning," but we're not. It's going feel like that because we're stuck in a cozy box of beliefs, handed down to us to perpetuate a nice but fruitless Christian life.

Believers are to be world changers, not world acclimators, in other words, thermostats, not thermometers. God wants to lay that box of beliefs aside, and He says: *It's all about My Son, My Spirit, and My Word.*

If you think you've got it all together and are content that God exists only to be your sugar daddy, then this book is *definitely* not for you. To follow what you are going to learn (in this book) about God and about yourself will seem like space travel because you have to leave your world to enter His.

I had to do the same, but that came after multiple failures and challenges that (thank God) forced me to see my *franchise faith* and "my world" for what it was: empty, fruitless, powerless, insecure, and of no benefit to God's kingdom. None.

In my heart and deepest yearnings, only one thing would satisfy: **Jesus.** When I was broken, Jesus was there, and with Him, I also met the Father and the Spirit because They are One. There was no church that could, or should, stand between Jesus and me. *Why had it taken me so long to realize this?* Why would I ever go back to the religion (or denomination) that dared to place itself between Jesus and me with its programs, meetings, and entertainment?

There was a betrothal between a franchised religious denomination and me. I needed to divorce from church-ianity to get married to the true Bridegroom. The Law was my schoolmaster to bring me to Jesus, but the church was my *ringmaster* to redirect my passion for Jesus to the church itself. *How pathetic is that?*

I sense you are like me. You no longer need a schoolmaster, and you definitely don't want a ringmaster. You just want a loving, secure, honoring relationship with *the* Master—Jesus.

Just so you know, each chapter in this book ends with me daring you to (maybe) push beyond your comfort zone . . . your world.

May God use this book to help you enter into the grace and joy of your Master.

Mike

P.S. Are all churches ringmasters? No, just most.

Part 1

THE BLANK CANVAS

1

FROM MY HEART

HI. I'M MIKE MOORE, a businessman from Texas. For starters, let's divorce *the way we think,* **not** our spouses.

The world is looking for hope, and it's not in a building, it's not in an institution, it's not the way we set the game up today. We set this game up to be played a certain way, and God gets in our face: *Don't play this game (of life) with your rules because I'll completely flip the rules on you . . . there are none for Me! There are no rules. You want to please me?*

Believe. *Believe what I say. Believe (have faith) in My Son.*

Honestly, I have more questions than I have answers. They may be your questions too, so keep on reading. *Holy Spirit, I can't see me the way You see me. Would You just change me in the way You want to change me?* We want to impart that in our home, in our community, in our business, at the Starbucks we go to, or in the gro-

/ 3 /

cery store. We want to love that worker who makes a mistake on the cash register and charges us five dollars too much—not want them to lose her job after we chew her head off because we almost lost a whopping five dollars. *C'mon man*, we are focused on the wrong stuff! That's why churches won't be filled up—because people want what's authentic, what's genuine, and what's real.

We must force out our old thinking and this judgmental box that we roam around with. We are the followers of the Messiah! We're a few good men and women . . . we're to be part of the Marine Corps for God, but too often we're not.

When I had a Bible study (I was with the Navigators), I memorized Romans, Titus, the Sermon on the Mount, Proverbs 1–5, many psalms—big portions of Scriptures. If God was looking for a few good men, I was one of them. I was married (miserably) and didn't know how to love, but I had Bible studies, and people were looking up to me to learn.

Once, a guy in my Bible study confided to me that he was in a marriage headed for divorce. I took him aside and said, "Number one, if you get divorced, you're out of this study group, and number two, if you go through with divorce, you need to seriously consider whether you're really a Christian." That's it. No love from me, no compassion, no encouragement, all judgment.

Later, he got divorced and was out of the Bible study. A year later, I moved to Dallas with my wife. Know what happened next? She and I got a divorce! We're at a courthouse where the judge's gavel had fallen to legally sever our marriage. I'm leaving the courthouse, and the Lord says to me: *So Mike, tell Me: are you a Christian? Are you a believer?*

That was too much for me, so I put my Bible on a shelf and said, "*I'm done!*" The Lord immediately said to me: *No, you're just beginning because now I get to show you My grace.* So I swung the pendulum the other way and said, "OK, God, how good is your grace?"

I tried everything, and it just kept coming back to grace and grace and grace. I understood (at this stage of my life) what it meant to live by faith and live under grace (under the new covenant).

Jeremiah 31 says that God has written His laws on my mind and on my heart (my desire center). He's put in my heart (who I am) that I *want* to do that. We don't know that, but we *want* to follow God. We *want* to listen to our Father, we *want* to please our Father.

The more I walk in grace, the more I understand that I want to obey my Father, not because it's some rule but because I want to be so close into His face that my face changes. In 2 Corinthians 3:18. it says: "beholding Him, we are changed from glory to glory." The English word *glory* is a translation of the Greek word *doxa* that actually has many meanings in Greek. In the passage above, *glory* means *opinion*.

We're changing from our opinion of ourself to God's opinion of us. That's what changes us—seeing what He sees, not what we see. When we see what He sees in us, we change. Behold Him. That's how we walk in the Spirit; we just behold Him: "God, You're Good.

What can I do? I need Your wisdom. I need wisdom every morning. Give me Your wisdom, Lord. Give me Your Spirit. I don't know what to do. I'm in the flesh. I'm in this body. Don't let me make rash decisions.

You made me the way I am. You wired me the way I am, but I don't know what to do here."

We cry out, but we look at Him. We behold Him like the Old Testament King Jehoshaphat in 2 Chronicles

He said, *Lord, we got this army coming. We don't know what to do, but our eyes are upon You.* A prophet later said to the king, "Because you looked at Me, you won't have to fight this army. Send the praisers out." Send the harpists and the guitar players out in front of the army, and when all this army comes out and sees these musicians, they're going to be asking, "What in the world?" Even the Hebrew soldiers said, "What? Are You kidding? We're going to go worship? That's our battle strategy?" You've got to have faith to go into the same boxing ring as Floyd Mayweather with only a flute, and he's coming at you.

To honor the Hebrew king's faith in Him, God had the opposing army destroy themselves. *That's what I'm talking about.* When we behold Him, we change.

Remember what God said: *Because you looked to Me, you won't have to fight this battle.* How many nasty battles in your life have you fought when you could have looked to the Lord and see Him fight for you?

We find people in some behavioral "no, you can't be that way" funk. It's attempting in the flesh to tell others how to live. Let's get them in the presence of God to behold Him. *Let God change people, and let us be content to love people.* God, not the church, is in the changing business; we just present.

We present people to Him and Him to people. This is like presenting offers in business (deals and mergers and acquisitions). A professional deal maker's job is to take and present offers to buyers, not to tell them what to accept. Present the offers, and when they see how amazing the offers are, they get to make the choice. It's the same way in our walk with Jesus. We present offers, we present truth, we present the goodness of God. We present people to Jesus, and God does the changing, not us. That's the bottom line. When people say, "I quit going to church," we have to separate the people, the building, the institution, the religion (and all it entails). We have to separate all that from God. We have to determine where the value lies. Does the value lie in God, or does it lie in the church? *Where is our hope?* Our hope is in God. Is our hope in what He says, or is it in the denomination? Is that where our hope is? And the peripheral is: "Yeah, it's God, but our pastor is up there and he went to seminary to learn the Scriptures, and he teaches that to us—but I'm not going anymore."

We're not really turning from God; we're turning from the church, and we're turning from people (that aren't walking in the Light). We're not turning from God because we were never next to Him (in there) to begin with! If we had been with Him, we might not have ever attended that church in the first place. Let's know Him as He wants to be known, not the way people want us to think He is.

As a little boy, my mom and dad would go on occasional weekend getaways. They didn't have much money, but my dad wanted to take my mom away when he could. They would go to a motel called 50th on the Lake on Fiftieth Street, at the lakefront, in Chicago. My mom would take us boys to spend the weekend at the home of Aunt Violet, an Italian woman. To my five-year-old perspective, I saw her eyes as dark, she wore black clothes, and she scared me big time.

Aunt Violet worked at a funeral home. So, when we went to her house, it smelled like flowers and like a funeral home. Even to this day, when I attend a funeral and smell the flowers, it reminds me of Aunt Violet. She would take the flowers that were thrown out (after the funerals) and bring them home. There'd be a big heart of flowers with a message like "I'll Miss You, Hal" or "Dolores, My One and Only." She'd have the flowers of dead people in her house. Is that morbid, or what? She kept her drapes closed, and it was dark. Frankly, I was afraid of Aunt Violet. She freaked me out.

At her dinner table, Aunt Violet would have my brother and me eat turnips. I tried to say I couldn't eat them, but she forced us to eat them. As a result, I hated turnips because they reminded me of Aunt Violet.

Fast-forward to the college I attended with an athletic scholarship. I'm in the cafeteria going through the line, trying to get what I need. I got to know the ladies behind the counter. I used to sweet-talk them: "Margaret, you're my best server. If I were older, I'd marry you." I was saying all these things because I needed more food than the regular portions. I'd get to the meat section and say, "Margaret, slip me another one."

She would say, "Mike, I can't do that. Everyone would want two."

"Put it under the potatoes or something."

And she did. Next, she reached over to put turnips on my plate.

"Margaret, I do not eat turnips. I will not eat turnips. Do NOT put turnips on my plate."

"What's wrong with turnips?"

"Nothing, Margaret; no turnips." There is nothing wrong with turnips, but they reminded me of my experiences with Aunt Violet. So I didn't want turnips.

Later, in my forties, I learned I'm supposed to be concerned about colon cancer. One of the foods that reduces the risk of colon cancer is turnips. So I read about turnips and started to eat turnips to get healthy. Now I can eat turnips!

What happened? There was never anything wrong with turnips. Turnips were always turnips. God made turnips. They always taste the same, and they were good for you. What was wrong was *what I associated with turnips*. There's nothing wrong with turnips.

It's the same way today with God. There's nothing wrong with God: *For God so loved the world* Jesus was sent to save the world. We tend to associate God with the bad experiences of the "Aunt Violets" in our past and present. It may be the church, the institution, the priest, the pastor, the rabbi, or the people. People turn us off, and we're associating God with that. What we need to do is separate the institutions and the people from God. Let God's character stand by Himself.

I DARE YOU to divorce from the belief that when you left the church you were leaving God. You weren't leaving Him. You left the things, like hypocrisy, that sent you in a trajectory away from God's love and presence. The one who hurt you is not God. I repeat: *God is not the one who hurt you.*

> The Romans tried to make Jesus into an institution. The Greeks tried to make Jesus into a philosophy. The rest of Europe tried to make Jesus into a culture. Finally, America tried to make Jesus into a business.
> **– Torben Søndergaard**

> "And whatever house you enter, stay there, and from there depart. And wherever they do not receive you, when you leave that town, shake off the dust from your feet for as a testimony against them."
> **– Luke 9:4, 5**

May you be the kind of person you want to fellowship with: mend the hurting with your love and your listening ear, feed the forgotten, forgive those who need forgiving, and encourage the brokenhearted.

DIVORCING THE LAW

IN ROMANS 7, PAUL IS WRITING mostly to Jews (those who know the Law) and tells them that the Law is in effect only for those who are alive to the Law. Here's his example: if a married woman has sex with another man, she's an adulterer. She committed a sin against God because she was married and had sex with another man. However, if her husband dies, she's free to remarry. (I love what Paul says.)

In the same way, we were made to die to the Law through the body of Christ, so we can be joined to someone else; we can be remarried. We can now be married to Jesus because we died to the Law and the Law died to us.

Check this out: Jesus was Jewish! I'm sorry, but He was not a Christian. The Christian church does not own Jesus. He is not owned by anybody. He is the Son of the Most High God. So Jesus, being Jewish, could not be married to someone divorced. Likewise, we are not divorced from the Law, but we have died to the Law. Therefore, it is dead to us. With the Law being dead, we can become the bride of Christ. We're not under the Law; we're under grace. The same spirit that raised Jesus from the dead dwells in us (His believers and receivers).

Side note: Jewish high priests could marry only a virgin. That means that the bride of Christ (His church) must be a virgin. How can this be resolved? Simply. When we come to Jesus, we are a new creation; "the old has passed away" (2 Corinthians 5:17). That "new creation" *is* a virgin. We are pure in His eyes, and He is free to be our holy Bridegroom!

He is not betrothed to a widow or a divorcee; His bride is a new creation!

So Jesus is going to marry a perfect, pure bride that is not merely divorced from the Law but is also dead to the Law. Because of that, we are now joined together with Jesus—who's been raised from the dead. THAT is powerful because now we are *in Christ*. It says in Hebrews 10 and Galatians 2 that by ONE sacrifice, not only are we dead to sin but also we've been crucified with Christ and we no longer live, but Christ lives in us. By that sacrifice, not only are we dead to the Law, but also we are joined to Jesus. It says by one sacrifice we are also sanctified. *Sanctification is not a process.* It is an event of receiving a gift!

Maturity is a process.

A baby pulled out of the womb is as human as a one- hundred-year-old person. There's no difference in their humanity. One is not more human. The only difference is maturity. *When we go to Christ, we're justified. We're sanctified (we don't have holy bodies yet,) but God puts the Holy Spirit in us.*

When we pray, "Lord, give me more love . . . give me more patience," God says: *I'm unable to answer that prayer. I've given you all the love, all the joy, all the peace, all the patience, all the goodness, all the kindness, all the self-control I can give you—it's the Holy Spirit that dwells in you. You already have all those things.*

When we walk by the Spirit, whatever we do in the flesh dies because the Spirit overtakes us. We need to know we are already sanctified—and walk that out because we're not only divorced from the Law but we're also dead to it. If we have to disregard our self to regard Jesus in His fullness, then bring on the disregard!

The Law was never given for justification of sin. Rather, it is the magnifying glass that makes us see the sin on our lives. What does Scripture say?

"The law of the Lord is **perfect**" [emphasis added]. That means there is no imperfection because you can't be both at the same time. What, then, is the purpose of the Law? It is "**reviving** the soul" [emphasis added] (Psalm 19).

Because the Law exposes sin in our lives and forces us to recognize it, we desire to be converted from a life of sin and bondage to a life of holiness and peace, in a word, grace. The Law is a schoolmaster that brings us to Christ. It doesn't justify us to Christ; it simply brings us to Christ. He is the one who justifies. The Law was never meant to be the tool to fix us.

First, it is the tool to show us that we are broken and unusable for the kingdom of God. Second, it is THE tool for our *sanctification*.

We never use a toothpick to try to remove a hubcap and loosen the lug nuts that secure our wheel to an axle. It is entirely the wrong tool for the job.

Conversely, we would not use a tire iron to pick something out from between our teeth. It is the right tool to change a tire but the wrong tool for dental hygiene. OK? Because the toothpick is incapable of removing lug nuts does not mean we should get rid of the toothpick. We'll need it to clean our teeth someday.

THE LIE of the enemy (in our day) is to throw the Law out altogether because we are now under grace. In essence, the New Testament church is saying, "Because we can't fix our tires (be justified) with God's toothpick (the Law), we won't look to it anymore. Therefore, our teeth go *unsanctified.*" But satan is OK with us going halfway (justified, but not sanctified) so long as we remain unfruitful for God's kingdom.

My human nature, my flesh, my feelings override who I am most of the time. I've got to let the spirit- man say, "I need to love that brother, Lord. I don't have that feeling for him, and I'm not sure I believe it. But the truth that is my spirit (who I am internally) attests to me that You love him; therefore, I love him. Just because I don't feel it doesn't mean it can't be that way."

It helps for me to verbalize it, to say it out loud. I don't need to feel the feelings. I love that man, and I can pray blessings on him and favor on him. And I pray, "God, You give him all his heart's desire and lift him up and encourage him and speak to him with kind and gentle words," because that is who I really am and that is what's true (in me) about that person in front of me. When we believe our feelings, it's not who we are. *We don't walk by emotions.* We walk by faith.

I have a friend that's a pilot with American Airlines. He's a check airman for the Triple Sevens. He told me, when he was in pilot training, he was taken up in the clouds where he couldn't see. At that point, the instructor said, "Close your eyes, and I want you to straighten the plane out and get it to normal." My friend did as instructed and let the instructor know when he was finished. The instructor said, "Open your eyes."

When he did, he saw they were tilted 30⁰ and were headed for planet Earth! They would have crashed. The instructor's point: If you rely on your feelings and not the instrument panel, you're going to crash. You've got to rely on what the instrument panel says. With that, my friend utilized the instrument panel and got the plane on a correct course, but he said, "I feel like we're upside down." The instructor said, "The instrument panel will not lie, but your feelings will." Friends, our instrument panel is the Word of God. It will not lie to you.

I DARE YOU to divorce from the Law(s) in your life and living by your feelings. Start speaking God's truth (verbally) about yourself and the people around you! Stick with the instrument panel He's given you so you won't crash and burn.

> Your emotions are very unstable and should never be the foundation for direction in your life. Wisdom always waits for the right time to act, while emotion always pushes for action right now!
> **– Joyce Meyer**

> *For the law of the Spirit of has set you free in Christ Jesus from the law of sin and death. For God has done what the law, weakened by the flesh, could not do. By sending his own Son in the likeness of sinful flesh and for sin, he condemned sin in the flesh.*
> **– Romans 8:2-3**

May you judge yourself and others by the instrument panel of God's Word, knowing we are dead to the Law and made alive in Christ through grace.

3

MAKE THE PAST NOT LAST

LIKE A COMPUTER, we carry our past with us every day of our lives. We even dream about the past in our unconscious state. Everything we ever messed up, every problem at school or work, and every person we wronged or disappointed in some way is stored in the vast petabyte hard drive called our brain. I trust you are reading this book with an eye to the future. Hopefully, you seek a life with a clear conscience before God and others. You're tired of the things that seem to defeat or deflate you. You are ready to walk on higher ground and abide in mountain-top experiences that will forever change your personality, your outlook, and especially your destiny.

Do you know what's holding you back? Do you know why you haven't gotten to take that victory lap in life's stadium? For me, I couldn't run because I was carrying too much on my back. Like the character called

Christian in the allegorical classic *Pilgrim's Progress*, I bore too heavy a load (or burden, as Christian would call it) to even pretend to run. That load was my past failures.

Those all-too-retrievable failures made me open season to the enemy of my soul, and satan had me where he wanted me, living under the shadow of an imperfect past. It didn't matter that I was a professed, baptized, born-again Christian. The enemy couldn't change any of that, but he was scary-effective at getting me to take my attention from my identity in Jesus and my title to a residence, accessed by streets of gold and abiding back in the dung heap of my past screw-ups.

The minute you come to Christ and say, "I surrender to You, Jesus, and repent of my sins," the enemy begins his campaign of undermining your victorious life. Your past is his favorite weapon. He uses it over and over again. *Hey, why mess with success?* Just about the first time you're ready to knock on a neighbor's door to tell him about Jesus, the enemy reminds you of your worst "door experience" as a kid—some kind of rejection or meanness or fear of a big German shepherd lunging out and taking a piece out of you. Then, you chicken out. Score: 1 for satan, 0 for loving your neighbor.

I can't change your past. This book can't change your past. No book can change your past. It is what it is, right? But it also ain't what it ain't. What it ain't is the death spiral of your future. Maybe it wasn't any screw-ups you made in the past; maybe it was people who messed you up big time. They disappointed you, they defrauded you, they defamed you, they defiled you (even if it was just once). Ever since then, the pain train has stayed on the tracks. You are living on *emotional life support*, and the devil has his foot on your air hose, saying, "Choo-choo, ding-ding," reminding you the pain train is still rolling. He tells you that you are powerless to stop it. "Don't even think about it," he warns.

Can I take just a second to remind you that he is a freakin' liar? Jesus calls him "the father of lies" (John 8:44). Jesus wasn't just name-calling; He's trying to give us a wake-up call! Every lie that has ever been told by anybody has the devil's fingerprints on it!

Have you ever driven under or around the lighted guardrails at a train crossing as a train quickly approaches? *Of course not.* That would be almost certain suicide.

Jesus reminds us that the enemy lies to us when he tells us there is no guardrail. Sure, there will be pain-trains coming through our lives, but we do not have to be in their path! We CAN let them roll by as we exercise a bit of caution (and a lot of faith and patience).

Everyone's got stuff in his or her past. So what? Who cares? Once you belong to Jesus, it has NO bearing.

Your past sins and failures are no longer factored in. It is written, "As far as the east is from the west, so far does he remove our transgressions from us" (Psalm 103:12). Your sins and mine have been sent to a place so infinitely far that they would be impossible to reclaim. Not happening!

There's a perspective on our past I like from a Hindu proverb that goes something like: "Your past problems were a life lesson, not a life sentence." I love that because a life sentence is exactly what the enemy wants us to live under. DON'T LISTEN TO HIM!

It is not his jurisdiction to place us (any longer) in condemnation and defeat. In other words, he no longer has a badge! He is no longer your authority; he is not your master. When you submit to Christ, Jesus is your Master, and you will stand before only His judgment seat. God's Word says Jesus is our Advocate, but don't lose sight that it also says He is our judge! The gospel of John says: "For the Father judges no man, but has given all judgment to the Son" (John 5:22). WHOA! That is a game-changer!

As the enemy tries to dump old crap on me, I can remind him (out loud) that I serve Jesus, and He is the only Judge.

Remember the disciple Peter? Was he perfect? Let's see, he nearly drowned when he took his eyes off Jesus. He basically told Jesus, "You ain't washing my feet."

And, oh yeah, he denied knowing Jesus three times in a row! And you think you are a screw-up compared to the disciple Peter? He is Exhibit A that Jesus loves us in spite of ourselves. That's huge!

So don't live life with a petabyte of destructive memories and past failures. Instead, use your Peter-byte of memory to recall how Jesus loves you as you were, as you are, and as you will be.

Here's the good news:

> But God, being rich in mercy, because of the great love with which he loved us . . . made us alive together with Christ . . . and raised us up with him . . . so that in the coming ages he might show the immeasurable riches of his grace in kindness toward us in Christ Jesus.
> **– Ephesians 2:5–7**

A person made alive with Christ has been ordained to live a life of good works. We tend to think of good works as something we do for others, but if we fail to do good works for ourselves, then we will face unnecessary obstacles to doing good for others. What good work do we need from ourselves to ourselves? *Commit to staying in the arms of Jesus.* He embraces us, and we must commit to rest in that . . . to rest in Him!

I DARE YOU to divorce from your past. Commit to be aware of Jesus embracing you for *three days*.

That's all. I mean really live it out: thank Him, love Him back, tell Him how secure you feel in His arms. Say to Him, "Hold me tighter" when things get rough. You are so precious to Him. *He wants to do this.* He has loving arms to hold you and the biggest shoulders to cry on. May you be swept up in His love today, tomorrow, the next day . . . for eternity!

> Though our feelings come and go, [God's] love does not.
> **– C. S. Lewis**

> *"I will not leave you as orphans: I will come to you."*
> **– John 14:18**

May you embrace and experience the exceeding riches of God's grace and kindness through Jesus Christ!

4

FEAR SUCKS

RECENTLY, I HAD TO CATCH a flight from Dallas to Portland, Oregon. It was a business trip to meet with a major corporation (whose motto is Just Do It).

Can I be real with you? When I fly, I don't like sitting in coach. If I had never sat in first class, maybe it wouldn't matter, but I have sat in first class and appreciate having more space to go over my papers and to organize my things and my thoughts. When that's taken away, it just stifles me. Who wants to go back to a rotary phone when you can use a touch pad? Or dial-up versus Wi-Fi? Same deal. I just feel less productive with less space.

When I booked the flight, my seat assignment was 17A! That is in the economy seats. In the middle of the night before the trip, I had a dream that I was going to have an anxiety attack on the plane. Have you ever had a panic attack? Some women refer to it as being

Great! I board this plane and sit in seat 17A. It is a window seat. As I am sitting there, I start to feel that anxiety I sensed at three o'clock in the morning, like a caged animal might feel.

I realize what is happening and tell myself, *This is crazy.* I send up an arrow prayer, "Lord, You're bigger than this. You're bigger than my feelings. The blood of Jesus covers this." Holy Spirit takes me to Philippians 4:6, "Do not be anxious about anything." Afterwards, I rebuke this funky panic, saying, *I'm not believing this. This is BS*, and I just relax.

Soon, a guy from India sits in 17C (the aisle seat). I introduce myself, and he cordially tells me his name is Kuran. We're talking, and I ask him if he would rather sit at the window. He says he's "an aisle guy." Bummer. I'm an aisle guy too, stuck in a window seat! So I wonder out loud, "I wish I could get an aisle seat somewhere."

Then, Kuran recognizes my need and says, "Why don't we just switch seats, Mike?"

"You serious?" I say.

He unbuckles, stands up to let me out, and gets into my seat.

Now I'm sitting in the aisle and feeling a bit relieved and grateful God put this guy in my row. I'm fine now.

The plane completely fills up, but before they close the door of the plane, the guy from the gate desk walks up to me and asks if I am Kuran (so and so). I tell him we switched seats and he's at the window. So, he says to Kuran, "Sir, may I see your ticket?" Kuran gives him his ticket, and he glances at it and then hands him an envelope. Turns out Kuran was first in line for upgrades!

The airline guy leaves.

Kuran looks at me and says, "Do you want this?"

I look at him and say, "What is it?"

"It's my new ticket, I've been upgraded to first class."

"Are you kidding me?"

"No, no you take it."

"Dude, that's *your* upgrade," I say.

He just reaches over and says, "Here."

I take my wallet out, retrieve two one-hundred-dollar bills, and extend them to him.

"I can't accept that," Kuran says.

I say, "You have to if you're giving me this seat." Now, I'm sitting in first class . . . and it gets even better because God says to me: *How far do I have to bury something for you to know I can resurrect* ANYTHING? You think you needed to be first. I put the guy next to you, who was first, and then he offered you his seat.

Can you grasp what I experienced on that plane? *The unmerited grace of God!* I didn't deserve to be upgraded; only the guy who was first on the list deserved that. He was the only one qualified to get an upgrade on that plane, not me. I was fortieth. *But God* heard my prayer, saw me tested by anxiety, saw me rebuke that to seek His rest, and heard me invoke the blood of Jesus as my battle cry. I have a great Father. He owns it all. A first-class seat is no biggie with Him. *So why wouldn't I ask Him for it?*

I just shared my mental battle with you, but there was a spiritual battle too. Did you see it? As 2 Timothy 1:7 reveals: "For God hath not given us the spirit of fear; but of power and of love and of a sound mind" (KJV). OK, God's word is telling me that fear is a spirit! I thought it was an emotion, but it is a spirit that plays itself out *through our emotions.* Wow! *What are we supposed to do with this new knowledge?* Does it give us an advantage we didn't have before?

This verse isn't about just what God *hasn't* given us but also what He *has* given us! He has given (past tense) us power, a spirit of love, and (as if that's not enough) a sound mind! Folks, *He's giving us what we need!* Who doesn't need His power? Who doesn't need His love? Who doesn't need a sound mind?

Legally, we need a sound mind to carry on business, to sign a contract. If we didn't have that, the contract would be void.

First Lady Eleanor Roosevelt once said: **"No one can make you feel inferior without your consent."** I'm here to tell you no one can make you fear without your consent. Like me, it may show up in the form of stress, anxiety, or panic, but that is the time for us to focus on God: who He is, what He's doing for us, how He loves and cares for us. It's all about Him! Because God is more interested in the relationship, not the reward. Unfortunately, I have a tendency to look at His hands (the gifts and rewards) instead of His heart. Are you the same way?

I hate formulas as much as I hate rules, but I do like simple reminders so I don't have to think things through all over again. When you experience fear, why not give new meanings to the letters of the word?

Focus on God, not your feelings.
Examine your heart.
Ask Him for good things.
Rebuke the enemy's fear, then receive God's loving mercy, and rejoice in the outcome.

Some people do the first three things right but stumble on the last. Be willing . . . no . . . be expectant of the good things you ask of God. Don't disqualify yourself as unworthy. *Just being God's child makes you worthy!* God had to teach even the apostle Peter to not call someone or something unclean if God calls it clean! *Just loving Jesus makes you clean.* You don't do it; He has already done it all. There is NOTHING left to be done that Jesus hasn't done. He said: "It is finished" (John 19:30).

I DARE YOU to divorce from your worst fears by approaching one thing that causes you fear. For example:

Strike up a conversation with a stranger. Unplug your electronic ball and chain (cellphone) for a day or more.

Give something that's special to you away. Ask someone to help you with something. Try something that's new to you—Thai food, playing an instrument, art, a new language, maybe something crazy like public speaking!

I'm telling ya . . . you can do this! I wish you could feel the confidence I have in you as you're reading this. Hey, if I can do it, you can too! Bottom line: *we trust God to do all the heavy lifting.*

Fear is worth divorcing. When you leave its grip, you will be a new person.

> Fear makes strangers of people who should be friends.
> **– Actress Shirley MacLaine**

There is no fear in love, but perfect love casts out fear. For fear has to do with [torment]. Whoever fears has not been perfected in love.

– 1 John 4:18

May you (in unwavering faith) trust in the love and power of God and permanently be divorced from a spirit of fear because when the fear leaves, the torment has to go too.

5

KILLING THE NEED FOR GREED

EVERY HUMAN BEING HAS a talent inside him or her. I don't know what yours is, but it's there. When we meet people, *everybody* is fighting a battle we know nothing about. I don't care who you are or how much money you have; you are fighting a battle no one knows anything about.

We have talent in us, and it's like people don't know what their talent is because they're so busy wanting to make money. I see a talented musician or a talented car mechanic, although he may be a neurosurgeon making three million dollars a year. Surgery is a job for him, but he'd rather be working on an automobile or playing music; that's his passion . . . and his true talent.

Too often, we sacrifice our talent for money. Of course, we have to make a living (don't get me wrong), and sometimes money funds our talent. We're so money-focused in the United States, versus most of the world where people are happy making just enough money so they can spend more time with their family. If your household takes in thirty-five thousand dollars a year, guess what? You're in the top 1 percent of wealth in the world! During the Occupy Wall Street unrest, thousands of Americans were demonstrating against the wealthiest 1 percent. The irony of it all is that (on a global scale) *the protesters are the wealthiest 1 percent!* It helps to know that.

This fact doesn't make us any better than someone else in the world, but it realigns our perspective.

Getting back to talents, how do I cultivate a talent so that when people see me, they say, "He's been with God?" not because I'm holy but because there's something different—I'm spending time encouraging people, pulling the treasure out of other people.

God sees your treasure when most people only see the dirt. That must be the way God really is! Not a God sitting up there with a whip, waiting for me to do the wrong thing. *It is the goodness of God that leads people to repentance* (which is changing their minds about who God really is).

If anyone tells you that money is the root of all evil, that is not true. A one-hundred-dollar bill is amoral. It is not evil in and of itself. It's just a piece of paper that we can exchange for one hundred dollars' worth of goods and services. The LOVE of money . . . that's where the evil lies. Why is that evil? Because we misdirect our love to a false thing. We cheapen the purpose of love when we love things devoid of eternal worth. That's why God loves people like you and me; we are of eternal worth! God's smart enough to know it.

We too easily fall in love with the minors at the expense of loving the majors: parents, siblings, children, grandchildren, friends, neighbors, anyone in need of your love. In God's economy, love is only reserved for people—not food, not alcohol, not clothes, not sports, not even chocolate. Remember, we cheapen love when we apply it to the wrong objects.

Another thing greed robs us of is humility. Jesus used two words to describe Himself. Do you know what they were? *Meek* and *humble*. First off, His meekness is not a wimpy thing; it is *power under control*.

Meekness is not weakness! The finest black belts in the martial arts are disciplined to be meek. Why?

Because if they hadn't learned meekness, there'd be a lot of mangled bodies out there—people who'd offended a black belt (knowingly or unknowingly).

At His crucifixion, Jesus had all the power to rain fire upon his Hebrew accusers, the Roman soldiers, and the people mocking Him, but He didn't. Instead, He said: "Father forgive them, for they know not what they do" (Luke 23:34). *That's real-deal meekness.*

That's power under control.

Being lowly of heart is the essence of humility. We tend to think humility is for losers because we've seen people humbled in sports, in business, at school, and in politics. That's worldly humiliation. But godly humility comes with quiet, confident power that few ever achieve.

Let me tell you about a humble man I met in 2018. His name is Datuk Edward Ong. Never heard of him, right? Be honest. If you're not familiar with Southeast Asian cultures, let me explain that Datuk is a title of honor, not a first name. If the base guitarist for the Beatles was a Malaysian, he'd be known as Datuk Paul McCartney, not Sir Paul McCartney.

I met Datuk Ong in Singapore, but his business is in Malaysia. His dad was a successful real estate developer, and Datuk Edward Ong learned the business from his father. The development business can be rather ruthless. Datuk Ong recalls: "We were very issue-driven and did not have people in mind. We just did what we needed to do, and when we had to bully someone, we would."

As I recall, he left the family business to start his own with enthusiasm. But at age fifty-nine, the 2008 real estate bust hit, and he lost $450 million and everything else. Even his wife left him. His response was to get alone with God for one week. Even though he'd lost everything, he got one message for sure: *Edward, you can't lose your salvation!*

God told him: *I will rebuild this fortune, and more, if you do business by Me, by My Holy Spirit, by revelation. Just wait on Me and let Me guide you.*

Datuk Ong had nothing, so he did that.

Today, he's worth $1.5 billion. He's the most humble, humble man. He's all about Jesus. He says: "You want to do business [with me]? We're going to talk about Jesus." He built the largest five-star resort in Malaysia they'd ever seen. Datuk Ong did in Malaysia what they did in the 1960s to Singapore— turned a garbage dump into an international destination city. He built the "Pride of Borneo" in the Malaysian city of Sabah.

Datuk Ong starts every day in prayer with his staff, hundreds and hundreds of staff. Muslims come to those prayer meetings because he's not converting anybody—they're just bringing honor and glory and praise to Jesus. Second only to the government, he's the largest employer in the area with about 1,800 people working for him.

This is a man that loves people, not money. Yeah, he's got a lot of money now, but part of humility means never forgetting there was a dung heap that God took him out of.

I DARE YOU to divorce yourself from greed. You can never own greed; it always owns you! So, for your own sake, let it go.

But Mike, it's too big to let go. It's how I hope to get ahead—get that big break I've been waiting for. OK, fine. It's your insurmountable object; I get that.

In business, when I observe people looking for a big break they can't get to honestly and with integrity, they break the rules till they get broken—sued, arrested, disbarred, voted out of office, divorced, you name it—all in the name of greed.

The main catalyst for greed is dissatisfaction. You show me someone who's greedy, and I can guarantee you they have issues with being not satisfied or content with elements of their life or lifestyle.

> The way we live is the consequence of the size of the God that we believe in.
> **– Datuk Edward Ong**

> *But [sinners] lie in wait for their own blood; they set an ambush for their own lives. Such are the ways of everyone who is greedy for unjust gain; it takes away the life of its possessors.*
> **– Proverbs 1:18, 19**

May you embrace satisfaction and contentment. Do not give up on your dreams and preferable future, but put it all on God's altar and begin to work towards those dreams with God as your (active) senior partner. To be free of greed is to be free indeed!

6

WHO DIED AND MADE YOU JUDGE?

MEN WILL NEVER UNDERSTAND what it feels like to have a baby. White guys will never feel what it's like to be Black, what they go through. I can try to understand, but I don't know what it's like walking down the street with black skin and what that feels like. Why? *Because I'm not Black.*

Years ago a white journalist did what could be described as a reverse–Michael Jackson, in that he took drugs to make his skin dark. He became a white man in dark skin (not blackface). He wrote a book of his experiences entitled *Black Like Me*. But even still, it was not the real deal because he was missing the experience of growing up in that culture. As I said, I can't know what it's really like to be a Black man.

I'll never know what it's like to be Latino.

I'll never know what it's like to be down and out and homeless.

I'll never know what it's like to be in prison for years and have freedom again. I do know what it's like to be in prison in my soul. We're all felons; it's just that some of us have been convicted of a felony.

I'll never know what it's like to be a police officer at the morning roll call and hear one of their best friends got shot in the face by pulling over a guy who was drunk.

We'll never know unless we experience these things, with all the implications, consequences, memories, and challenges that result. We have so many opinions, we have so many feelings, and we have so many judgments about things *we know nothing about*. We react and join these resistance movements, and we think this is all new? It's been around for two thousand years!

As I write this, thousands of people have recently taken to the streets of many US cities to protest (via riots) over the death of a Black man named George by a police officer in Minnesota.

It's impossible for me to make a judgment about a group of people I know nothing about, which means I need to divorce myself from the opinion that I know what they go through and how they feel . . . because I don't.

How do we live life understanding other people? How do I live so I truly care about (actually *love*) the person sitting in front of me?.

Why are we at odds with other people? What fuels the arguments we have with others? Why does our society embrace labeling others, name-calling, and canceling?

Case in point: also as I'm writing these thoughts, the US Senate is considering a judge named Brett Kavanaugh for becoming a new US Supreme Court justice. He's had about twelve hours of testimony before the Senate Judiciary Committee, and then right before they are to vote (yay or nay), a woman from his past shows up and alleges he wronged her in college.

Immediately, the battle lines are drawn: some hold that she's a slut or a publicity seeker and discount her story as a specious fabrication; the other side wants to believe her story (for various reasons), makes her into some brave, heroic #MeToo icon, and considers the judge a misogynist cad, unworthy of being on the Supreme Court. There you have it!

There's a difference between a *debate*, an *argument*, and a *discussion*.

I'm debating when I say, "That's *your* opinion." (In fact, half the time, I'm not even listening to your opinion because I'm waiting to get my opinion out.) In a debate, every word is filtered to make sure it is *just right*. You not only articulate your point, but you also surgically dissect the opponent's point to make the person look ridiculous and unbelievable. There is no room for concession in a debate: you're right, the other is wrong.

An argument is an emotional exercise, often devoid of logic. There are no filters, to speak of. That's why when we argue we tend to say things we regret later—or even instantly if it hurts the other person deeply. In discussions, we have to first articulate the view and opinion of the other until we understand the person.

When we disagree, we can't say, "Well, I believe (such and such)" because that doesn't matter. What we can say is: "*If what you say is true, then what about this?*" Now I'm in a discussion. The key to it is being willing to change your mind if the other person is making sense to you.

What about the line, "Let's agree to disagree"? My first question is: What are we disagreeing on? Our belief system? A fact? My experiences in life versus your experiences in life? What is the disagreement about? Because *we can't disagree on facts*.

A disposable cup is a container made out of plastic, foam, or paper. We *can agree* on facts like that. We can have *a discussion* on what we could drink out of it. We can *debate or argue* as to which one is better to drink out of. What is our disagreement about? Why would we even call it a disagreement? Former Democrat senator Daniel Patrick Moynihan wrote a letter to President

Richard Nixon which said: "You are entitled to your own views, but not your own facts."

God is the God of love, but He is also a God of clarity. He makes it clear that judgment belongs to Him, that revenge belongs to Him and not us. *"Vengeance is Mine; I will repay,"* He says. That means we cross a line when we take it upon ourselves to get back at someone. It really is silly when we stop to think about it: She took something from you, and now you want to take something from her; he called you a bad name, and now you want to call him a bad name on Facebook or write on a public woman's restroom wall "Tony is an @#*-hole!!!"

The door of forgiveness was never even cracked, but the door to an ongoing feud is flung wide open. *How you respond to Tony says a lot about you.* It's not about him! It's about you and your willingness to do your part to fix that relationship.

Taking matters of vengeance into our own hands is a form of idolatry because we express unbelief or dissatisfaction with God's promise to repay in His way, in His timing.

I hate to admit it, but when we make ourselves judge, jury, and executioner, we are giving God the finger. There's no other way to dance around that reality. I don't know about you, but God is the last one I want to give the finger to, right? He's the last one I want to rebel against or turn away from (by my actions).

I get that people hurt us. *Been there, done that.* It's easy to feel hurt when someone's looking down at me and making me the butt of his or her jokes. The person can try to make me feel inferior, but at the end of the day, as I quoted Eleanor Roosevelt earlier, I am the captain of my feelings. *I decide* whether I leave a situation any less tall than I was at the beginning.

Sure, if I stole something from you and you call me out on it, I need to feel remorseful but not inferior. It is the perfect opportunity to test my will and integrity to make it right with you. A little personal responsibility, combined with a heartfelt "I'm very sorry," goes a long way. The trust may come down the road, but the respect is instant when we make an effort to restore the relationship with those we wronged, or who wronged us.

A dude comes up to you in the parking lot of a grocery store. He says his car broke down on the way to take his daughter for her kidney dialysis and needs twenty dollars. This is a time for you to judge whether he's truthful or going to put that twenty dollars into his meth or booze fund. This is a matter of discretion and discernment. It wouldn't hurt to send an arrow prayer up to God and say: "What should I do?" After that, you go with your gut—trusting that God is letting you know one way or the other. But whatever your gut says has to line up with Scripture to truly be of God.

One test is based on the fact *God loves a cheerful giver*, so if you grudgingly pull out that twenty-dollar bill under obligation or pressure, you can be sure it is not of God. When doing something makes you feel dirty or exploited, it was not God's doing.

On the other hand, if this encounter rises to the level of a divine appointment, it becomes a privilege to give the money out because Jesus says, *As you give* "to the least of these," *you are giving to Me.* Wow!

Have you given twenty dollars to Jesus this year (in the form of someone in desperate need)? Maybe it's time to let God turn our hearts of stone to hearts of flesh and enter into the compassion of God.

How do I divorce myself from judgment? *I've got to know how God doesn't judge me when I screw up* and desire to be more like Him. God gives us not a license to sin but the *permission to fail* and run back to Him.

I DARE YOU to divorce from judging others and give them some grace.

> God loves you unconditionally, as you are and not as you should be, because nobody is as they should be.
> **– Brennen Manning**

> *So then, as we have opportunity, let us do good to everyone, and especially to those who are of the household of faith.*
> **– Galatians 6:10**

May grace abound in your heart and on your lips as you learn the habit of blessing others with your words and not criticizing or judging.

7

MY PRIDE IS BETTER THAN YOUR PRIDE

WHAT CAN REMOVE A QUEEN faster than a New York minute? **Pride.** The ancient Persian queen's name was Vashti. Her husband, the king, was Ahasuerus. He was the bad, bad Leroy Brown of Persia (if you're a fan of the late Jim Croce): "Badder than old King Kong / And meaner than a junkyard dog."

As tough as he was, the human in him let his pride obscure his judgment. One week, he threw a big (guys-only) party, and the Who's Who of Persia were there to celebrate and get drunk. In that state of being, the guests asked the king to summon the queen. Why? Because she was a drop-dead gorgeous woman and the guys wanted to ogle her under the pretense of obeisance to the royal family.

So, King Ahasuerus called for Vashti, his trophy wife, to come (the less clothed, the better). She was busy with her own ladies' event when the order came through.

She knew they were drunk by now and how the men would stare at her, so she did the unthinkable . . . she said no.

Her impertinent response was quickly conveyed to the king in front of his honored guests. All eyes were on Ahasuerus. It was not his idea in the first place, so maybe he'll let her be. No, his pride was wounded, and he became enraged. Then his wise men exhorted him: "Oh mighty king, this cannot be. If Queen Vashti gets away with refusing you, then all our wives will get the idea they can do that to us too!"

So what started out as guys just wanting to enjoy looking at Melania (I mean Vashti) morphed into a power struggle between all the husbands and wives in the Persian world!

As a result, servants were deputized to search out the lovely women in all the provinces to find a replacement for Vashti. One was found, and Vashti was not only dethroned but forbidden to ever appear before the king again.

What was once a solid relationship was cut off due to the husband's pride (and lack of ability to protect his wife). She protected herself, and that hurt his drunken, fragile pride. By the way, the king came to power through Vashti's father. Ouch!

How about your kingly pride? What pushes your buttons? Maybe it's correction of any sort: how you should drive, how you should speak (or refrain from speaking), how you grow your hair, the clothes you wear; whatever. The acid test of whether we're prideful is our response to these assaults of our character and personality.

Like fear, pride is a spirit, a very strong spirit. How do we deal with strong spirits? With the strongest spirit in Heaven and Earth—God's Spirit. We enter into Holy Spirit's power when we confess our sins to God, in this case, the sin of pride. There is a God- initiated covenant in 1 John 1:9 that says: "If we confess our sins, he is faithful and just to forgive us our sins, and to cleanse us from all unrighteousness." (Yay, God!)

I DARE YOU to divorce your pride and put it on God's altar of mercy. Let it go. Receive His cleansing. Only He can activate the wash cycle and hit the rinse button, right?

It is hardly possible to overvalue ourselves but by undervaluing our neighbors.
– Lord Clarendon

One's pride will bring him low, but he who is lowly in spirit will obtain honor.
– Proverbs 29:23

May you take your pride for a long walk on a short pier and never bring it back home to your thoughts.

Part II

BEGINNING TO SKETCH

THINK YOU'RE HAVING A BAD DAY?

I DON'T MEAN TO MAKE LIGHT of anyone's challenges and difficulties. That would be simply wrong, so let's pretend I'm having a bad day and I feel bummed out, frustrated, maybe helpless, and in need of some kind of do-over or something.

Whenever I begin to invite myself to my own pity party, I need to think about the David who slew Goliath. When he was no longer a boy, he became a fugitive of the jealous king of Israel (Saul).

One day David, his family, his army of six hundred men, and their families were encamped in a town called Ziklag. David and his men went out to battle, and as they returned to Ziklag, they were horrified to discover the enemy (Amalekites) had swooped in while they were gone, captured the women and children, taken all the good stuff, and burned the city to the ground.

History records (in 1 Samuel 30) that David's men all wailed and cried till they didn't have any strength (or tears) to continue their group anguish. Then, their anger turned towards David. *He was in charge, so he must be responsible for this.* All of them were ready to kill him.

This is what I compare my bad days to: spouse kidnapped, sons and daughters kidnapped, all valuables looted, house and city burned to the ground. As if that weren't enough, six hundred tough guys are fixing to hang me or stone me to death. You see, I can't imagine a worse day. Put another way, my worst days are nothing compared to David's day in the smoldering ruins of Ziklag.

If you're like me, the main goal is to simply survive such a day, to make it to tomorrow. Of course, David wanted to survive, but how? He called the priest to facilitate inquiring of the Lord. He asked God if there would be any point in pursuing the marauders. *Would they be killed? Would any good come of it?*

God assured David that he and his men would prevail, not just win a battle but also have every loved one restored safely and even get their stuff back (plus a lot more spoils of the enemy!).

It was too good to be true, but that was all he needed to rally his troops to retaliate and rescue the hostages. Let's not miss the fact that David had to make a life-or-death decision based on what a man told him God said! That takes guts.

So they began an unknown journey until God had them find a servant of the enemy that was left in the desert to die. David's group revived the man, and he gratefully told them all where to find the enemy camp. *Do you think that was an accident?*

God is providing for David; He's our provider too. Indeed, David and his men hit the enemy with a surprise attack, and their efforts were blessed by God—they did get their families back and much more to boot! (Yay, God, again!)

So what does this account teach us? It teaches us to not give up, to accept that things of great value to us may come in small, unusual packages or circumstances. Finally, trust that what the Lord reveals is His plan for you. He is never wrong, and He never loses a battle, let alone a war.

David's key was to "encourage himself in the Lord" (1 Samuel 30:6, KJV). It was after doing this that he summoned the priest, inquired of God, and received the assurance of success. The $64,000 Question is: *How do we encourage ourselves in the Lord?*

When we hear the word *encouraged* or, another way to say it, *strengthened*, let's consider other places in Scripture where these words are mentioned and see if we can detect a pattern.

The apostle Paul wrote a letter to the church at Philippi, like the church in Dallas or the church in Phoenix or the church in Tampa. Here's the church in Philippi, and he says, "I can do all things through Christ which strengtheneth me" (Philippians 4:13, KJV). Through Him, we're strengthened (or encouraged)! Exactly what happened to DAVID! He was encouraged/strengthened in (or through) the Lord.

There was another person who used the word *strength* in the Scriptures as well. His name was Nehemiah, and he had a very unique career. He was a sommelier, or wine expert. Back in the day, they were called cup bearers to the king. It was a dream job, tasting wine all day, but I digress . . .

Nehemiah says this in Chapter 8:10, "the joy of the Lord is your strength." There it is again, so now we have three references concerning being strong in God or encouraged or strengthened. So let's look at them and put them together.

1) David, *he strengthened himself in the Lord.*
2) Paul: *I can do all things through Christ, who strengthens me.*
3) Nehemiah: *The joy of the Lord is your strength.*

Let's look deeper at this verse in Nehemiah before we move on. It is not my joy *in* the Lord but the joy *of* the Lord. *What does that mean?* It means the Lord's joy is my strength, not my joy in Him. It's Jesus's joy. It's God's joy, and that joy is my strength. Wait a minute! How does someone else's joy provide me with strength?

Let's camp on the word *joy*. What is this word *joy*? In Hebrews 12:1–2, it says: "Since we are surrounded by so great a cloud of witnesses, let us also lay aside every weight, and the sin which clings so closely, and let us run with endurance the race that is set before us, looking to Jesus, the founder and perfecter of our faith, who for the joy [there it is!] that was set before him endured the cross, despising the shame, and is seated at the right hand of the throne of God." There's a joy set before the Lord Jesus.

It says He "endured the cross." That preceded the joy of the Lord (the Lord's joy, as spoken in Nehemiah). So we say: *That's my strength?* Nehemiah is telling us, *When I look at the Lord and I see His joy, then I'm strengthened. I have to see His joy first, not my joy in Him, but His joy. That's what strengthens me.*

There was joy on the other side of the cross. What happened at the cross? Jesus took away the sins of the world: past, present, and future! He is the Lamb of God that takes away the sin of the world (our sins).

What happened at the cross? Jesus became the Lamb of God, the last Lamb, the only Lamb. That Lamb was to die only once, never to be repeated.

As Peter said in 1 Peter 3:18, "For Christ also [died] once for sins, the righteous for the unrighteous, that he might bring us to God, being put to death in the flesh but made alive in the spirit."

What was that joy then? He endured the cross and gets to the other side and here's the joy. The joy set before Him was that He could look back and say: *Not only did I take away your sin—past, present, and future (which brings Me joy)—but when you look at Me, you know I'm the God that forgives and I will not hold your sin against you.* As it says in 2 Corinthians 5:19, "*In Christ God was reconciling the world to himself, not counting their trespasses against them.*" God was in Christ. He teaches: *I don't count your sin against you. Man may, your friends may, your spouse and kids may, your employer may, but I won't. I won't hold your sin against you because Jesus died for it. If that wasn't sufficient, then He's not My Son.* Friends, Jesus's blood is sufficient, poured out one time for you and me.

THAT IS OUR STRENGTH IN LIFE! WE ARE FORGIVEN! Period. DARE TO BELIEVE THIS!

So let's recap. Here's David strengthening himself in the Lord. David understood the heart of the Father.

He understood God is such a forgiving God that there's nothing man could do that God couldn't forgive.

So then, *what does it mean to strengthen yourself in the Lord?* It means sitting down and understanding (at a heart level) that, when Jesus died at the cross, one act of obedience to His Father (according to Romans 5) reversed the curse that came upon mankind.

In one glorious act, God said, *In Christ, all your sins are gone.* Understanding that will strengthen us.

That's our strength. There's unspeakable joy in really knowing your sin is gone in God's eyes. But that joy is just a down payment. The real deal is to enter into the same joy Jesus had after His cross experience. His joy!

When we understand the depths of the covenantal transaction that occurred at the cross, when we get that, our inner person will be strengthened!

Now, we don't see this in Scripture, but I promise you David said, in his heart: *Lord, I killed a giant, and that feat was all You. You were with me, and I've been following You. I know you're a forgiving God. You're not holding anything against me or these men for being angry at me.* When he got right with God (internally), the strength was manifest as David now had the kahunas to say: *Guys, put your swords on.*

We're going to go and get everything back. God said we're not losing anything!

In Jesus is the forgiveness of sin, not judgment. **In Him** is the blood shed for us, not judgment. **In Him** is love, mercy, joy, peace, and the Holy Spirit, not judgment. **In Him** is everything we need pertaining to life and godliness.

When we go into God (into Jesus), if we feel at any level that we are judged, we are not being strengthened in Jesus. Guilt is the proof. Jesus is not going to bring our sin up! That is not Jesus. The Spirit of God will move us to the cross and empty tomb to say: YOU'RE FORGIVEN! From whom, then, do you need to ask forgiveness?

Let's move on. Stop beating yourself up because your Father in Heaven beat Jesus enough. Forty lashes with a cat-o'-nine-tails for your healing! Then He was taken to the cross, and we don't know how many times it took to beat those nails into His flesh: pounding . . . pounding . . . pounding.

When we do not accept His forgiveness of sin, we are really saying: *Those whippings, those beatings, those thorns penetrating Your scalp, those nails in Your hands and feet, You shedding your blood are just* **NOT ENOUGH!**

We may try to excuse it and say: *I'm just repenting and I'm feeling bad.* If you're feeling bad, **you are trying to atone for your own sin!** There's a godly sorrow that's different from us feeling bad in our conscience—

bothering us for a behavioral pattern that God's already forgiven us for.

We have to be able to discern between the two (godly sorrow vs. worldly depression/pity parties). That's how we strengthen ourselves in the Lord.

I DARE YOU to divorce from feeling unforgiven. Take time each day this week to thank Him. Rest in that. Soak it all in so you can have the power and desire to divorce from the feeling-bad-about-your-last-failure BS . . . which is called self-atonement. You know what to do about it: CHANGE YOUR THINKING! Jesus experienced all His trauma both *for* you and, to be honest, because *of* you; but we don't hate ourselves for crucifying Jesus. Instead, we love Jesus for experiencing real judgment and death so we won't ever see a judged person again when we look in a mirror.

> Grace means that all your mistakes now serve a purpose instead of serving shame.
> **– Brené Brown**

> *For I know the plans I have for you, declares the LORD, plans for welfare and not for evil, to give you a future and a hope.*
> **– Jeremiah 29:11**

May you be quick to encourage yourself in the Lord during life's darkest times. May HIS joy be your strength, and **may you** never forget that you can do all things through Christ—who strengthens you.

9

EXTRACTING THE PRECIOUS FROM THE VILE

I'VE BEEN THINKING A LOT about extracting the precious from the vile—how difficult it is to extract gold and silver from mountains and coal from tunnels, the lengths that human beings will go to mine minerals. They go deep, deep, deep into the mountains, risking their lives, just to get coal to use as fuel and for various other uses. If humans can go to that length (because they see the value in what's hidden inside), how much more does the God of the universe desire to extract our preciousness and lead us to understanding—that *He died to save us*.

What does it mean, that He died to save us? What's the end game in God's mind? It's not for us to modify our behavior but to see that He changed our entire identity (from the inside out), which will produce godly behavior, right living, and the desire and power to do His will.

God's Word introduces us to a woman named Rahab, who was a prostitute in a town called Jericho. Her "home business" was in the fortified wall of the city. To live in the wall is like having a luxury condo. But then, consider her lucrative occupation.

As the Israelites are conquering Canaan, the next city of conquest is to be Jericho. Two Hebrew spies are sent to recon the city and report back to Joshua, their commander.

When Rahab meets the Hebrew spies, she says (to paraphrase Joshua 2:8–11), *We know your God is God. Our hearts fainted and melted within us when we heard how your God parted the Red Sea, and how He killed and destroyed the Amorite kings.*

Consider this: when God had Moses part the Red Sea to escape the approaching Egyptian army, it was forty years prior to her meeting these spies. She wasn't even born yet! How did she know this? Where did she get this information about God, to make such a statement? TV? Internet? *Jericho Gazette*? TikTok?

No, none of the above. She heard by word of mouth. All her life she's heard this, probably first as a little girl at the dinner table. As a kid, she must have been thinking: *Oh my goodness, that's the one true God!* I can imagine her looking up at the stars and saying: *You're real, but Who are You?*

Fast forward to her meeting the two spies. She could tell they were Hebrews, but they weren't the enemy to her. They were her personal missionaries—sent by the God she always wanted to know! Her local king was told the spies were at her place and sent his men there, but Rahab risked her life to safely harbor the Hebrews from being captured. She even suggested to the spies how they could best escape!

As a reward for her extraordinary cunning and boldness, she and her father's household were spared from the utter destruction of the wall and the entire city. God saw the precious in Rahab when others saw only the vile. He SO accepted her that she is in the very lineage of Jesus!

Over one thousand years later, Jesus is alone at Jacob's well in Samaria and is approached by a Samaritan woman. They have a discussion. Back then, women from Samaria weren't supposed to talk to Jews. Jesus was a Jew (and considered a rock-star rabbi, at that!), and He asks her for some water. She says: *You're a Jew who's not supposed to be talking to me*, but she draws Him water. It's late in the day, and she's out there alone because she's an outcast from the other women in town. Why? Because this gal is one of "those women."

So they get into a discussion, and Jesus starts talking about living water. She replies: *Sir, where can I get some of this living water? What is it?* Jesus says: "Go, call your husband and come here" so they can discuss it. She says, "I have no husband." Jesus says, "You are right . . . for you have had five husbands, and the one you now have is not your husband. What you have said is true." She looks at Him and says: "Sir, I perceive that you are a prophet" (John 4:16–19).

Jesus didn't judge her. He didn't belittle her based on her stating the obvious (*You're a prophet*). Then she goes on: "Our fathers worshiped on this mountain . . . I know that the Messiah is coming (he who is called Christ)." Jesus tells her: "I who speak to you am he" (John 4:20, 25–26). She drops her water things, runs into the town, and tells everybody because she's been changed from the *inside out*. Jesus invested His time with her to extract the precious from the vile.

She was the town hussy, the one who never met a guy she wouldn't sleep with, so the "honorable" women canceled her. (You talk about cancel culture; here it is!) This same woman, the outcast, became a one-minute missionary for Christ—and her mission was the town she lived in and even the men she had cohabitated with. Many townspeople came to Christ because of her. Jesus spent a few days there, and many more received Him as Messiah.

At what point did Jesus scold the woman about her adulteress affairs? *Never.* He was not focused on making her stop the evil in her life but was all about her starting a new life in Him! We are certain her evil ways ceased because darkness cannot abide with light, and now, for the first time in her life, she had the light of Jesus in her and her preciousness flourished!

During the Roman occupation of Israel there was a Jewish tax collector named Zacchaeus (we'll call him Zach). Actually, he was the head honcho tax collector in town. Back then, Jewish tax collectors (for Rome) were the lowest of the low in the community, yet among the wealthiest. They were hated because they constantly took advantage of their official position and extorted tons of extra cash for their own benefit from the Jews.

It was a very lucrative gig, and we can be certain that all the other tax collectors gave hefty *baksheeshes* (bribes) to Zach to keep their jobs. In Texas, we'd say that these tax collectors were lower than a snake in a wagon-wheel rut. (That's pretty low!)

Anyway, Jesus comes to Zach's town of Jericho. (Side note: it had been rebuilt since Rahab's time when God destroyed it but spared Rahab's family.) There is a throng of people all around Jesus as He is walking a certain path. Zach had a problem. He had heard about this amazing rabbi with miracle powers and wanted to see Him, but he was not tall enough to see Jesus at ground level.

Looking down the road, he spotted a tree and quickly ran there and climbed it for a good vantage point to see Jesus walk by. When Jesus came to the tree, He looked up and summoned Zacchaeus to come down and go home to prepare a meal for Jesus! This was done, and Jesus later became Zach's honored guest. The crowd grumbled about the company Jesus was keeping. *Why . . . Zach is a sinner!* At no point during the meal does Scripture record that Jesus told Zach to "make things right." He didn't have to because Zach had an encounter with the Holy One of Israel, and his heart completely changed!

At some point, he declared to Jesus: "Lord, half of my goods I give to the poor. And if I have defrauded anyone of anything, I restore it fourfold." How did Jesus respond to all this? He said: "Today salvation has come to this house" (Luke 19:8–9).

Zach lived a vile life. He was like a Mafia don, exploiting Jewish taxpayers of their hard-earned money year after year. The town saw his actions and hated him for it, but Jesus saw his heart and *loved him in spite of his actions.* Jesus saw through the vile and found the precious in Zach. He just needed a God-encounter to draw out the preciousness of his heart. We don't get to see the faces of the poor folks getting blessed by Zach returning his ill-gotten gains in the days and weeks that followed. We don't get to see the surprised look on the faces of those that got, let's say, four hundred dollars from Zach because he hustled them out of one hundred dollars. (What do you want to bet that at least one of them was among those that murmured about Jesus hanging out with a sinner?) God has a sense of humor and irony, but more important, He has the ability to see the precious in all people, even you and me!

I DARE YOU to divorce from seeing only the vile in people. Look deeply for the precious in those you live with, live near, work with, go to school with, and hang out with, and see past the things you count as vile (their current or past behavior, the way they talk, eat, or dress). *Why?* Because like Zach and Rahab and the Samaritan woman, Jesus has done that for **you**.

It's simply seeing people as God sees them. Many years ago, singer Amy Grant had a hit tune called "My Father's Eyes." The chorus relates that God's eyes see the good in people when we cannot, that His eyes are full of compassion. I want eyes like that, don't you? Because if we don't look for the precious, we'll get distracted by the vile.

> For beautiful eyes, look for the good in others; for beautiful lips, speak only words of kindness; and for poise, walk with the knowledge that you are never alone.
> **– Audrey Hepburn**

If you return,
Then I will bring you back; You shall stand before Me;
If you take out the precious from the vile,
You shall be as My mouth.
Let them [your persecutors] return to you;
But you must not return to them.
– Jeremiah 15:19, NKJV

May the spirit of Jeremiah become alive in you so that you will begin to see (with the Father's eyes) and extract the precious from the vile in your life and in the lives of others.

10

SATAN'S SPERM

THERE ARE A LOT OF WAYS this chapter could be taken wrong. The title seems like a dumpster fire in the making, but bear with me on this because the following is shockingly accurate.

Consider our minds are like the reproductive parts of young women and satan's goal is to impregnate our minds with lies. His sperm comes in many forms: lies in music, lies in TV shows, lies in movies, lies on the Internet, lies in school curricula, lies in the workplace, lies in books and magazines, and just plain lies from any source.

For instance, when a person goes into an adult entertainment bar, he gets knocked up (all night) by satan's sperm. It isn't being raped by satan; it's consensual. No one is forcing you or me to hang out there. Some of the lies he floats around are *Women are sex objects* (no they aren't!), *This is normal* (no it isn't!), and so on.

Let's look at this from two perspectives: the flesh and the mind.

In the flesh, God intended for reproduction to happen (whether it's in humans or animals) when a sperm meets an egg of a woman (in her womb); a zygote is made. A zygote is the beginning of human life.

There's life in an egg and life in a sperm cell, and when they come together, a zygote is formed, it attaches to the wall of the woman's womb, and the birth process begins—an AMAZING miracle.

In the mind, God also intended for reproduction to happen (by faith). The book of Hebrews says: "For unto us was the gospel preached, as well as unto them: but the word preached did not profit them, not being mixed with faith in them that heard it" (Hebrews 4:2, KJV).

So the Word goes forth. What's the Word? The Word is that life-giving substance, the sperm. What's the egg? The egg is our faith. When the Word goes forth and it's mixed with our faith, an amazing miracle happens. The Word has life. Our faith has life. When the two come together, something amazing happens. We're saved! Born again! God's child!

Things happen when we believe what God says. It comes together and a spiritual zygote is formed. It grows and it grows. It's amazing what God does. It's just like what happens in a woman's womb when a man's sperm (which is life) is mixed with a woman's egg (which is life): BOOM, a miracle occurs in that womb.

Now, let's talk about satan's sperm. It is not life; satan's sperm is death. He's a liar and that's all he is. He is falsehood and deception. Nothing he is, nothing he thinks, and nothing he says is anything other than complete lies, falsehoods, and deception. He is the father of lies. He is the originator, the source code, of deception and lies.

His sperm goes out under the guise of life. There's no life in it, but it parades itself as life. We say: "Wow, I believe that!" We take our belief (our faith), and we couple it with death. What happens next? There's a stillborn. There's a baby in our womb, and we feel: *Oh, this is amazing! I can't believe there's this life in me.* Everybody around gets excited, but eventually, it brings death. We look at what we believed. We look at what we put our faith in. It started with life, but we coupled it with death, and death was inside all along, and we didn't even know it!

The more of satan's sperm that gets into us, the more opportunities there are for one or more elements of his lies to take, so he spreads his sperm en masse.

That means a particular lying seed comes in contact with an "egg" in our minds, and sin is conceived.

Once sin has been conceived (as a thought), it gives birth to deception, whether in words or actions—all because we took in that seed.

The book of James puts it this way: "But each person is tempted when he is lured and enticed by his own desire. Then desire when it has conceived gives birth to sin, and sin when it is fully grown brings forth death" (James 1:14–15).

Do you see the pattern? First, satan draws a man to, say, look at some porn. Next, that looking conceives lust and then desire. That desire drives him to a local massage parlor. One day, he comes back with a gun and shoots the people there to death. Am I overstating Scripture? No, I just described what a twenty-one-year-old, named Aaron, did on March 16, 2021, near Atlanta, Georgia. He killed a total of eight people at massage parlors because he said he had a sex addiction and those places were, as he put it, "a source of temptation."

When we pride ourselves by thinking *This won't really affect me*, we are merely putting on a perforated condom to feel protected. Of course, that is not effective. The only way to keep unstained from satan's sperm is by abstinence. Never let it penetrate you. How? By staying away from the presence of that sperm.

When we stray from abstinence (by believing satan's lies), we are playing with fire. Scripture asks a rhetorical question: "Can a man carry fire next to his chest and his clothes not be burned?" (Proverbs 6:27) Even in the world, we are warned: If you hang around dogs enough, you're going to get fleas.

Let's not deceive ourselves about how well we can handle satan's sperm. The only reason (a complicit) Monica Lewinski got a stain on her blue dress was because of the character of the company she was with that day. It's too simple to not get stained, whether it's in our flesh or in our mind. *No sperm, no stain.*

How do we avoid the sperm of satan? We have to know what God says. We have to know His Word. His Word is life. "For the Word of God is living and active, sharper than any two-edged sword, piercing to the division of soul and spirit, of joints and of marrow, and discerning the thoughts and intentions of the heart" (Hebrews 4:12).

People say the Word condemns us. No, the Word has come to save us! A surgeon's scalpel can save a person's life, but you can use that same scalpel and take someone's life with it. The Word of God is used to bring life to us. When we know what the Word says, we can combat the attacks of the enemy because the enemy roams about like a roaring lion, looking for somebody to devour. Meaning what? *To believe his lies.* Couple his lies (sperm) with our starting to believe him, and it produces death.

The first time that sperm was inseminated was with Eve. All satan did was take and twist the truth, which made it a lie:

What? Did God say you can't eat from any of these trees? I can't believe He said that.

No, no, no, Eve replies, *He didn't say that. God said: "Don't eat from this tree or touch it."*

Really? satan says. *Well, what's wrong with it? I mean, God knows, if you eat it, you're going know the difference between good and evil. You'll be like Him! Why would He withhold that from you? I'm just saying, you know, it looks good to me.*

That lie, that sperm, came out, and Eve believed what he said, passed it on to Adam, and immediately caused death for the entire human race. Not just physical death, but death to where the Savior of the world had to come. God knew this before day one. The sperm of satan is dangerous. It looks pretty, it looks amazing, but the end is the way of death. *There is a way that seems right to a man;* that's when we believe the lies of satan, we receive that sperm, and we believe it. There is a way that *seems* right, but there's death; it's a stillborn birth. That's the sperm of satan. It cannot produce life; it can produce only death.

About six days a month a young woman can get pregnant, but your mind can take in satan's sperm any day or night to conceive unrighteousness. We need to get that. *I need* to get that and live my life accordingly.

Most of the sperm we take in is voluntary, but that is not always the case. Many innocent children and adults have had satan's sperm forced on them. That is spiritual (if not physical) rape. It is reprehensible and wrong on all levels. All we have to do is look at the amount of child trafficking around the world.

Here's the difference between the two ways the lies get to us. One, when we consent to being inseminated by satan's sperm (wrong thoughts/lies), we need (get to) ask God for forgiveness. *It's on us.* Two, when his sperm is forced on us, we need (ultimately get to) forgive the person(s) who put us in that position that left us feeling abused, disregarded, betrayed, or exploited. Either way, satan's sperm got to us. The path it took to get in us determines how we need to overcome it, by God's grace.

Sure, on an earthly scale, forgiveness is unthinkable and off the table, but we're talking God's scale now. It reveals that we need to forgive because we've been forgiven too. What does the Lord's Prayer say? "Forgive us our trespasses [sins] as we forgive those who trespass [sin] against us." That prayer asks God to forgive (cancel out) my messes in the proportion that I forgive the jerks that messed me over. I don't know about you, but I don't have the grace to forgive, say, a pedophile . . . but God does. He gives me that grace if I am willing to take it from God and apply it to others.

Years ago my friend Nick Vujicic spoke to over six hundred sex slaves (girls and women, thirteen and older) in India. To say their lives were a living hell is an understatement. Each day the sun came up, all they could expect from that day (and night) was to be raped over and over again. Their Indian masters paid seven hundred dollars to their parents when they were age ten. From before puberty, they got inseminated with satan's sperm, plus countless johns who had their way with them.

Nick's message of hope and the love of Jesus allowed a number of these slaves to get out of the organized brothels and get cleansed, be saved by grace, and be filled with the Holy Spirit.

They later were trained, learned needed skills, and then got jobs. They saved their wages until their savings reached seven hundred dollars. Guess what they did next? Each went back to the brothels and found the guy that took her out of her childhood home.

In her hand was a bucket of water and a cloth. She would go right up to the guy and say: "Do you remember me?" Then, she said she was there to tell him Jesus loves him and she forgives him of every vile thing he put her through. Next, she asks to wash his feet and begins doing so. For twenty minutes, most of the pimps cry like a little girl because of the undeserved grace they are receiving at the hands of one of their many victims.

Finally, she gets up and hands the man seven hundred dollars and takes a sex slave girl away with her.

This pattern was repeated (victim after victim). Two words: GRACE and REDEMPTION. We all need to receive both and, with God's strength, give both.

Hey, this is not an easy road. It wasn't easy going in, and it can be awful hard going out. At the end of the day, I'm concerned about your freedom, not their freedom. If I describe just you, I am so sorry for whatever you went through. When one of us hurts, we all should hurt. Jesus says we fulfill His law when we bear one another's burdens because His law is Love. Whoa! What a touchy subject, right? The word *offensive* comes to mind. Sometimes we have to be offended to face truth because we wouldn't get it any other way. In Jesus's day, the scribes, priests, and Pharisees were the holiest folks around (in their minds and by their outward actions). Then one day, Jesus looked them in the face and called them out as no one would dare do.

He declared they were "hypocrites" and "whitewashed tombs" and sons of their father, the devil! Jesus had obviously not read *How to Win Friends & Influence People*. No, His assignment, from the Father was to speak the truth to these men. It is no reflection on Jesus that they couldn't wrap their minds around His words. They were too arrogant to receive it and change their belief system and attitudes. Are we too arrogant to receive the truth of this chapter and change our beliefs and attitudes that result in us shacking up with satan (the enemy of our souls)? We need to ask ourselves: *Who's our daddy?* That's what Jesus was getting at with the hypocrites He was addressing. If satan is your father, then you either serve him or run away from him and get adopted by another Father.

Are you the daughter or son of a Holy, Righteous, Loving, Pure, Merciful, Forgiving Father? If not, why not? Why not come to Him right now? *Take a moment to pray an honest prayer to God and confess your sins to Him and ask Him to forgive you as you surrender your life to Him.*

Your adoption papers were signed in Jesus's blood. No one can take that away from you, *except you.* You choose whether to believe the lies like: *it's not real, I've done too many bad things, God's too holy to want me,* and on and on. He DOES want you. When you look in a mirror, God wants you to see Him in your face—radiating His love and grace. The peace you need in this life is on the other side of accepting God's adoption papers.

You've heard mobs in the street chanting, "No justice, no peace," but here's reality: *No adoption, no peace*. Step into the waiting arms of Jesus and be soaked in His perfect love and forgiveness. Peace has to follow.

I DARE YOU to divorce the habit of being used as satan's spiritual sex toy. Commit to be unstained by his sperm from now on.

> Education without morality, as useful as it is, seems rather to make man a more clever devil.
> **– C. S. Lewis**

> *Religion that is pure and undefiled before God the Father is this: to visit orphans and widows in their affliction, and to keep oneself unstained from the world.*
> **– James 1:27**

May you find your safe zone where you cannot be exposed to insemination by the enemy. If there is not a safe zone to be found, then may you create one with God's help. **May you** be cleansed by the blood of the Lamb from all satan's stains in your life, at every age, and in every circumstance. If any of those stains were not by your consent, **may God give you** the grace to forgive your offender(s) with the same fervor as those young women did in Mumbai, India. (By the way, in about three years, the human trafficking and sex slave brothels on that ten-acre compound closed for good!)

11

THE DEATH ZONE

SO MANY PEOPLE want to climb Mount Everest, but there is a death zone at the top. It's the last 849 meters. Everybody that succumbed there was a highly motivated human being, but they didn't make it. Maybe they didn't use a Sherpa.

What's a Sherpa? That's a local guide who knows the mountain. Sherpas are equipped to handle weather and other challenges. Before you climb Mount Everest, you sign a binding document and that document says: *Whatever the Sherpa tells you to do, you have to do it as instructed.* The Sherpa doesn't get paid if you come down in a body bag! That means, if you get to the death zone and the Sherpa says, "There's a storm coming; we can't go up," then you don't go up! They have water and food and oxygen to help people get through that last leg. If you are climbing Mount Everest, you are a fool to not depend on the Sherpa.

Life is like a tall mountain, and we are fools not to depend on God to see us through to the summit.

Better (life) climbers than you and me have tried but failed. They didn't think they needed God to make the climb, and the death zone is a testament to their foolish disregard for eternal life and salvation while on Earth.

You see, the death zone is the death zone for only those who aren't prepared. Worse yet are the climbers that *thought* they were prepared, only to realize (too late) they were woefully unprepared. The enemy of our souls wants everyone who does not have Jesus in his or her heart to *feel prepared* for eternity. But, without Jesus, you are not prepared and never will be! Cemeteries are filled with the remains of people who thought they were prepared to meet their Maker but were not ready for the Judgment Seat of Christ.

They all felt they were a good person while they lived on Earth. They could always find someone worse than them to compare themselves to. That was their fatal mistake. They compared themselves to other people, instead of the holy and righteous Jesus. They moved the bar so low that it was not possible for them to fall short of Heaven *in their eyes*. NEWSFLASH! Only God gets to set the bar. Only Jesus gets to judge our deeds, our thoughts, and our words. No one else has the right or authority to do so.

THE DEATH ZONE / 85

You know what? For those who are prepared to stand before the Judgment Seat of Christ, it's not a death zone for them. In fact, that Judgment Seat is their ticket to glorious, eternal presence with God.

I DARE YOU to divorce from thinking you are a good person just because you are not an axe murderer (or anything else). Instead, ask Jesus to be your Sherpa. He doesn't charge you and has already experienced the death zone so you won't succumb to it!

> I understand I'm a sinner. I'm not perfect, and I need a Savior, and that I'm not going to make it to Heaven on merits and doing good things.
> **– Matt Holliday**

> *But when the goodness and loving kindness of God our Savior appeared, he saved us, not because of works done by us in righteousness, but according to his own mercy, by the washing of regeneration and the renewal of the Holy Ghost.*
> **– Titus 3:5**

May you be prepared to face death and the death zone by your knowing Jesus and Jesus knowing you.

12

PAUL IS NOT THE NEW MOSES

IT CAN BE SAID that Moses points us to God as the Lawgiver (though not at the exclusion of grace) and Paul points us to God as the Gracegiver (but not at the exclusion of the Law).

God talked about His law and our sin in the books of Jeremiah and Hebrews: *I will write My law upon your heart, and your sin and your lawless deeds I will remember no more.* Ask yourself this: why do I remember what God has forgotten?

Now, let's take a deep dive in the book of Hebrews to see what God has to say about the Law and Grace. "For since the law has but a shadow of the good things to come . . . it can never . . . make perfect those who draw near. Otherwise, would they not have ceased to be offered, since the worshipers, having once been cleansed, would no longer have any consciousness of sins? But in these sacrifices there is a reminder of sins every year. For it is impossible for the blood of bulls and goats to take away sins" (Hebrews 10:1-4).

Here's the key: *For the Law can never make perfect.* ALL who try to follow the Law into Heaven fail.

In Hebrews 10:16–18: "This is the covenant that I will make with them after those days, declares the Lord: I will put my laws on their hearts, and write them on their minds . . . . I will remember their sins and their lawless deeds no more. Where there is forgiveness of these, there is no longer any offering for sin." "No longer any" means no more, nada.

Enter Jesus in Hebrews 9:28: "So Christ, having been offered once to bear the sins of many, will appear a second time, not to deal with sin but to save those who are eagerly waiting for him." We read that the Law can never make us perfect. We also read that there's no more consciousness of sin. We also read there's no more offering for sin. There's not a reminder of sin in Christ. There's not a consciousness of sin in Christ. There can't be. Under the Law there is, but not in Jesus.

Sometimes I may see a friend that's down in the dumps and ask, "What's going on?"

"I feel really bad."

"What did you do?"

"Well, I did this and this and this . . . I feel really, really bad. I'm moody, I'm down."

I ask: "Is that penance? That sounds like penance. That's exactly what you're doing. You've been forgiven, and there's no more sacrifice, so your fake mood is actually a sacrifice for sin because Jesus's sacrifice was not enough for you—so you have to feel bad or compelled to make up for it by fasting or trying to lead someone to Christ."

Whatever you do out of feeling bad because you sinned (to cover up that sin) is a *false work*. It's called an *evil work from an evil conscience*. Because the Word says "Where there is forgiveness, there is no longer any offering" (Hebrews 10:18). You can't bring an offering to God anymore. You can't offer anything to God for your sin—it's impossible.

Jesus was the final, the *only*, the perfect once-and-for- all-time offering for the forgiveness of sin. He died two thousand years ago and forgave Mike Moore for all his sin. I wasn't alive yet, which means ALL MY SIN HE PAID FOR WAS IN THE FUTURE. Not some of it, all of it!

Let's not get stuck in a time warp going, "Well, the Lord has forgiven me up to August 1, 2010, but come August 4, if I have messed up, I'm going to have to ask the Lord to forgive me." *He already forgave you for it!* Before you even conceived it, He saw your whole life and STILL accepted you and saved you at the cross.

THAT understanding . . . THAT depth of love . . . will change the human heart. We need to reflect THAT. The moon does nothing to reflect the sun. It just is.

That's all! Believers have to do nothing but reflect Jesus. They have to be and abide and remain in Him—looking at Him, talking about God, knowing they're forgiven. We are so SIN conscious. I think that breaks the heart of the Father. We must renew our minds to be FORGIVENESS conscious.

Think about your child sitting at the table for a meal and looking at you and looking at you.

Finally you say, "Honey, what's wrong?"

"Nothing."

You continue: "Is everything all right? Are you wondering if I'm OK with you?"

But she just sits there, wondering, "Did I do the right thing? Did I do the right thing? Is Dad going to be mad at me?"

You want to say: "You're my daughter, I love you. Just be yourself!"

When your children get that security of your love for them, it allows them to be who they are and not walk on eggshells all the time. How many times do we ask God: *Are You OK with me?* (when He makes it clear He already is OK with us)?

The guilty conscience wants to appease itself. That way we can live with ourselves. It's like an offering. If my conscience is barking at me and barking at me and I throw it a biscuit, that should calm it down.

God's saying: *You're trying to atone for your own conscience. You're trying to make atonement for your sin within yourself. You're trying to do something so you don't feel bad anymore.*

The best example (for that) is the List we carry around. There are certain things we don't think twice about, and we wipe our mouth when we do them (like nothing happened).

Case in point, a friend of mine took a college class (about ten years ago) and he didn't want to be in it because word had it the professor was *the worst*! His classmates told him to get out of the class, so he went to the registrar's office and told the registrar he was taking care of an elderly grandmother in the evening and couldn't do a night class, and she changed that class for him.

He came over to my house afterwards and was defeated. He felt bad, and I asked, "What's wrong?"

"Bro, man, I lied and I just feel so bad."

"Really? What happened?"

He told me the story.

I said, "That makes you feel bad that you lied to get out of the class?"

He said, "Yeah. Here I am saying Jesus is my Savior and I just lied straight up!"

"So you did attend one or two classes? Were there a lot of students in the class?"

"Yeah, probably thirty."

I said, "Any girls?"

It was summertime, and he said, "Dude, there was a girl, and she had on some short-shorts, and you could see her waist. She obviously worked out and was tan."

I asked, "How many times during class did you have sex in your mind with her?"

"Dude, probably the whole class." He's smiling and laughing about it.

I said, "You know what's interesting?"

"What?"

"That it doesn't bother you that you had mental sex and committed adultery with a female classmate, but it does bother you that you lied to the registrar. You are like every other human being on planet Earth. You carry a List around that *you think* notes right and wrong. You carry that with you, and if you violate what *you think* is right in your own conscience, then you go crazy and you try to make atonement for your sin."

So I asked: "How are you going to atone for your sin right now? What are you going to do? Feel bad the rest of the night? Maybe go to a 7-Eleven and tell somebody about Jesus or give out tracts? What are you going to do? *What you are going to do is going to hurt you more than what's already been done.* Jesus paid the price. HUMBLE yourself right now, get humble and say: "Lord I got nowhere to go other than to go to You and say, 'That's what I do, Lord. I lie to get out of a situation.' Just say it!

"And keep going: 'But, Lord, thank You that You forgave me. Thank You that the cross was enough. And, Lord, I don't want to do that again. I don't want to constantly lie to get myself out of situations. I need the Holy Spirit to help me speak truth and have self- control because that's my old nature; that's what I want to do to save my face every single time.'"

GET HONEST! God knows that. He knows you're going to do it AGAIN, and He's already forgiven you for it.

My buddy said, "Wow, bro, wow! You're right. I'm fornicating with her mentally, and Jesus said that if you look at a woman that way, you've committed adultery in your heart."

When you sin, the Law can't make you perfect. You're trying to be made perfect by the List you carry around—saying that if you do these five things or eight things or whatever's on your List, then you'll feel good about yourself. Those feelings give the false impression that you're in good standing with God.

But it's Jesus (and only Jesus) that puts you in good standing with the Father. It's the blood of Jesus, one time, once and for all, never to be repeated again. It's done!

The apostle Paul lays out a bunch of exhortations (not rules) to the saints in Ephesians 4:25–30:

> Put away falsehood . . .
> Be angry and do not sin;
> Do not let the sun go down on your anger,
> And give no opportunity to the devil,
> Let the thief no longer steal . . .
> Do not grieve the Holy Spirit . . .
> Let all bitterness and wrath and anger and clamor and slander be put away from you, along with all malice.

Some people want to read this as Paul giving us the new Ten Commandments, but he is not the new Moses. He is instructing the Ephesian believers in what it should look like to be a follower of Christ. Look at Ephesians 1 and 2 to see what believers are and have. Believers are:

> blessed with every spiritual blessing (1:3)
> holy and blameless (1:4)
> predestined (1:5)

> blessed . . . in the beloved (1:6)
> in him have redemption (1:7)
> sealed with the promised Holy Spirit (1:13)
> made . . . alive together with Christ (2:5)
> raised up with him (2:6)
> seated . . . with him in the heavenly places in Christ (2:6)

And believers have:

> obtained an inheritance (1:11)
> the eyes of your hearts enlightened (1:18)
> been saved, through faith (2:8)

It continues through Ephesians 3. And then, you get to "Paul's List" in Ephesians 4, and it says to put away all lies, speak truth, and so on.

After all Paul just said in the first three chapters, I gain a context for what comes next. But if you go straight to the List in chapter 4, it comes across as a law. *The church is making Paul to be the new Moses, but he's not.* Paul's not making new rules; he's exhorting us to live a life apart from the old sin nature. That's Paul's message to us.

Let's be a real-life example. Tonight, you may look in the mirror and see a sinner and question whether you're saved. That's not what God wants you to see. He wants you to see Jesus in the mirror because that's how God sees you—perfect.

Consider what the high priest would do with sacrifices brought to him under the Law. He would examine the offering for the sin of the person who brought the offering. He examined the (innocent) animal, not the (guilty) person.

God is not examining us. He's examining Jesus (who is the Sacrifice). If the Sacrifice is good, then you're all good. If the sacrifice is bad, then you're all bad. Examining the person is a non-starter because everyone knows he or she is coming with a blemish needing atonement for.

When we self-atone, we are looking at ourselves and not the sacrifice of the Lord. It's a game-changing, negative, self-fulfilling prophecy trying to self-atone. It all has to do with our feelings, and that's the enemy's playground (to concentrate on how we feel). The why behind the what (self-atoning) is that we don't believe what God says.

Friends, the only thing worse than what Adam and Eve did (eating from the Tree of the Knowledge of Good and Evil), is not truly and fully receiving the redemption and atonement of the blood of Jesus. *It's that serious.*

I DARE YOU to divorce from the *Me, Myself, and I* savior-complex that satan tries to embed in us. It leads to spiritual suicide when we try to atone (make right) what only Jesus made right on the cross. James 4:7 says, "Resist the devil, and he will flee from you," so we need to resist the temptation to self-atone.

> Trust wholly in Christ, rely altogether on His sufferings; beware of seeking to be justified in any other way than by His righteousness. Faith in our Lord Jesus Christ is sufficient for salvation. There must be atonement made for sin according to the righteousness of God. The person to make this atonement must be God and man.
> **– John Wycliffe**

> *There is therefore now no condemnation to those who are in Christ Jesus.*
> **– Romans 8:1**

May you focus on the Sacrifice (Jesus) and not on you. By doing so, **may you** bear no unnecessary pain, feel no unnecessary guilt, and experience no unnecessary loss that He has already completely paid for.

13

COUNTERFEIT CHRISTIANITY

COUNTERFEIT RELIGION is pervasive in the United States. Most people talk about counterfeit money. The Department of Treasury trains its officers to be counterfeit experts. I'm told they don't spend time examining counterfeit money. Instead, they devote their time to examining—touching—real Treasury notes. They can tell what's the real deal just by feeling it. Paper money is made up of 25 percent linen and 75 percent cotton. It has a certain feel, and they get so acquainted with the real that they can spot a counterfeit bill immediately.

We spend so much time (in churches) and point to others and say, *This ain't right*, and it's all about behavior, about what we're not supposed to do. That's a counterfeit Christian life. There was a movie, called *Chocolat*, about a fictitious, small, very legalistic French village. The mayor was a count, and he ran that village with an iron fist. We would call him a control freak. The

Catholic priest even had to run all his homilies (sermons) by the mayor in advance. The mayor would change the sermon to communicate his expectations of the people. Finally, at the end (spoiler alert), the mayor let the priest give his own message, and the young cleric declared to the congregation: "Let's not define our goodness by what we *don't do.*" That's what's going on here and now. We often define our Christian life by what we don't do. We give kudos when you achieve *the not doing*. I'll give you a medal because you haven't had sex outside of marriage in four years now. (Whoa!) You're in AA and have finally hit your one-thousandth day sober. (Wow, that's awesome!) We tend to reward ourselves for what we don't do.

For instance, if you haven't touched a drop of booze in ten weeks, the success isn't that you've not had a drink. The accomplishment is exercising faith and self-control for ten weeks. So when you tell me you mastered self-control for (a certain amount of time), it motivates me to exercise self-control and exercise my faith. I may not struggle with alcohol. I may be a binge eater or something else. If you haven't imbibed in weeks, I'll say, *So what? I haven't either.* That's basing our value in what we don't do. But if you do self-control and faith well, now I can try to apply that to my will and emotions to overcome my personal challenges in life.

Let me put it another way. The *what* is that you haven't had a drink in weeks, but the *why* is because you made a commitment to trust God and have your self-control override your historic desires. That's what we need to be focusing on.

Instead of what happens in *Chocolat*, why don't we reward each other for what we *do* do? Meaning if you believe Jesus as your Savior and Lord, WOW, there's a reward in that! (That's amazing.) *I just spent time studying grace and I memorized five verses.* (Wow! No kidding? That's fantastic!) Why don't we share THAT with people?

We get caught up in the counterfeit side of Christianity, and we miss the Lover of our soul. We miss the One that came and gave His life for us.

That's what we need to be focusing on—*what* He did, not what have we NOT done. By the way, *what did He do?* He removed all our sin: past, present, and future. That's what Jesus did! *That's awesome!*

WHY did Jesus do that? So we could be back in relationship with the Father and have a close, eternal relationship with Him. That's the *why* behind the *what*. We need to spend time with the *why*. Isn't the *why* behind the *what* the most important anyway?

For instance, why did God lead His people out of Egypt (after four hundred years of slavery)? To spend more time with them. That's what good fathers do. As a good Father, God said to Pharaoh: "Let My people go." Pharaoh resisted till God forced him into compliance. (God sent the plagues to Pharaoh not out of judgment but out of love, and He did the same for the world during the Covid plague.) The slaves were set free, and the Jewish Exodus began. Pharaoh (like the mayor in *Chocolat*) needed to learn the lesson that *he was not God.* NEWSFLASH—neither are we.

Listen, God is merciful, and He runs the universe—He owns it. Didn't the same thing happen with us? We can compare the Exodus to the coronavirus pandemic. In 2020, God said: *Everybody listen!* He stopped the world so He could have time with us.

Whatever you believe about the coronavirus, just know that God is in control.

For years, people were complaining and bitching: *Man, I work so hard. I wish I could be at home with my family and still get paid.* Well, God granted us our wish, and now we're going *Oh . . . gee whiz, the kids are driving me crazy. I've gotta get back to work!* It's complain, complain, complain.

That's who we are—complainers. Let's be real. Let's face the fact that we are a complaining group of human beings. We complain, and then we blame someone else for what's going on. God, in His mercy, shuts the world down because He wants to spend time with us. That's all. God says: *I just want time with you. Can you give Me your time?* What did we do with all that time?

It wasn't enough. You can bank on that. We just didn't use that precious time to get closer to Him, and now we're back to the hustle and bustle of life. God's just showing us His mercy. He wants to be intimate with us.

The counterfeit church deflects this intimacy with God (from the knowledge of the real—Jesus). You can call me anti-denominationalist if you want, but so many (well-meaning) denominations redirect their members' excitement and passion for Jesus and replace it with a passion for the denomination. It's partisan piety and denominational exceptionalism on display for the world to see. That turns people off, and it turns God off. Why? Because it deflects us from the goodness of God and gets us to focus on what we *shouldn't be doing*—behavior, behavior, behavior— which deflects us away from God's intimacy. It basically says to us: *OK, when we don't do these things, we're good with God.* No, we're not! God is not works-based; He is grace-based!

Anything less than grace-based is a counterfeit religion, it's a counterfeit Christianity, it's full of holes, it's BS, and it's not right. The enemy is using this in the church today to keep us away from an intimate relationship with the Lord Jesus Christ. Like a well-executed scam, we think it's a good thing to be all-in for the denomination and don't even realize how abiding with Jesus has been tossed aside. We completely buy in to the *bait and switch*.

Friends, we have to work at not getting caught up in that. We have to swim upstream, which takes intentionality and effort on our part. Going with the flow takes you right into self-judgment and the judgment of others. That's a non-starter when it comes to intimacy with God.

Of course, we want to be obedient to God's commands and the commands of Christ. Obedience flows from intimacy with God, but intimacy doesn't flow from obedience to God. It doesn't work that way. Let obedience be the by-product of your intimacy with your loving, all-powerful Father.

The take-away is this: *Don't sweat the small things!* Meaning if you focus on obeying the two major commands, all the minor commands will fall into place. Those major commands are (1) love God with all your heart, mind, soul, and strength, and (2) love your neighbor as yourself.

Counterfeit Christianity has you enslaved to mostly man-made rules with some scriptural commands thrown in there. They are *rule-focused* and not *grace-focused*.

One of the many litmus tests of whether you attend a counterfeit church is how it handles members and guests that are divorced, are homosexual, look or dress different, and so on—with grace and truth or with judgment and bias?

I DARE YOU to divorce from counterfeit Christianity (in yourself and those around you). Be the one that so loves God that His grace is on your lips, rather than complaining and murmuring.

> The hope is indeed that some will experience and believe: The purpose of a number of spiritual gurus is to demonstrate to God-fearing men faux spirituality.
> **– Criss Jami**

> *Beloved, do not believe every spirit, but test the spirits to see whether they are from God, for many false prophets have gone out into the world.*
> – 1 John 4:1

May your intimacy with God grow exponentially and not stop till Jesus comes for you or you go to Him at the final sunset of your life.

14

THE LOVE OF A PRINCE

HIS NAME IS PRINCE. He was a twelve-week-old puppy when I got him. His breed? A miniature pinscher (Min Pin). They don't get over ten pounds. I first met Prince at my breeder-friend's place. I had to wait six months to get him. She gave me all his papers, and I bought him a brass tag with his name embossed. When I saw him, I said, "OMG, I love him." I knew about him, but he didn't know me, so he was apprehensive at first. It's like God and us. He says: *Oh, how I love you SO much!* He knows us, but we don't yet know Him.

Even though Prince is little, he acts like he's a 150-pound Doberman protector. He'll get between people and me to guard me. It's hilarious. The first night, I put him in his crate in the family room, and then I went to bed. Well, that never happened again! He cried so much that now the crate is on top of the bed, and he's there with his blanket and toys, and I sleep soundly. At 4 a.m., he wakes me up to deal with his nature call(s) outside, and then we go back in to sleep a bit more. Wherever I walk, he walks. When I stop, he stops. Wherever I go, he's around, and if he ventures off a bit, he always looks back at me to make sure I'm still there, that I haven't left him. When I run outside to stay in shape, Prince runs along with me. When I'm at home, he just wants to be held by me. Isn't that what we all want? *To be held?* I mean a real, lasting embrace. I'm not talking about being held by a human being (although that's awesome when we want that and need that). I'm talking about being held by the One that made us—in an embrace that will last forever. When God embraces us, we know we're hugged by Him. That hug never dissipates.

In my experiences with Prince, I see the Lord saying: *Mike, this is how I want you to be with Me. I want you so tied in to Me as your source. You've accepted Jesus as your Savior. That's wonderful. That got you into the relationship with Me. Now, I want you just to look at Me. Enquire of Me, "Lord, is it OK if I take this trip?" "Is it OK that I go into this Starbucks?" "Is it OK if I move in this direction?"* That's not Law; that's not craziness; it's just being so intimately tied with the Creator of the human race that He wants to guide our steps. His love wants to move us in a Heaven-ward direction during our earthly existence.

I also realize something really important about this little puppy. It doesn't matter to him what clothes I wear. It doesn't matter to him how much money I make. He doesn't care what I look like. He doesn't care. All he cares about is me. Who is *me*? (Right?) What's *me*? I thought *me* was what I did. I thought *me* was my job. I thought *me* was my house, where I went to school, who my parents were, where I live, all my accomplishments in life. No, that's not it at all.

It's just the fact that I exist, and Prince shows me my value just by loving me.

Let's take NBA star Michael Jordan as an example. Does he have value? Of course! He's probably one of the richest athletes around. Wall Street would say: *Yeah, he's worth a lot!* But when he was one year old, he had no awards, he had no NBA titles, he had nothing but wet and dirty diapers!

Ask his mom if he was valuable at age one. Wall Street would tell you something different from his mom. Wall Street would say he wasn't worth much at all because he hadn't accomplished anything. He could not be monetized. But now, at age fifty-eight, Forbes values him at $1.6 billion! It's his persona.

When you take the *a* off *persona*, what do you have? A person. That's what an animal looks at. It looks at YOU. Animals take in you as only a person.

When God sees us, His love shines on us. *Oh the depth of the riches both of the wisdom and knowledge of God!* That we may know the love of Christ that surpasses knowledge. It surpasses our understanding, so God says: *Since you'll never be able to understand how much I love, I'm going to show you. I'm going to put in your life puppies or little babies or folks with Down's syndrome to show you how I do love.*

Author Brennan Manning said: "The closest you will ever get to understanding the unconditional love of God is when you see a disabled child without a normal IQ, and all they know to do is love." Puppies consistently love. Even when people mistreat them, they still come back with more love and devotion.

They just want to jump up and down and play. They learn your habits. That's what it's like. When we understand love like that (like a puppy), we'll want to please our master.

All dogs want to do is please their masters, to be OK with them. Is it any different with God? We pee and poop, and God says: *That's OK.* He (proverbially) cleans it up. There comes a point in life where He's training us to do it outside. When we're ten years old, if we're doing the same thing, wouldn't you think He would expect more from us? It's not about rules, regulations, and behavior modification; it's receiving instruction from our Heavenly Father. He knows best how we function.

Here's another example. Warren Buffett is one of the wealthiest investors in the world today and is president and CEO of Berkshire Hathaway. What was his net worth when he turned five? Fifteen? Twenty-five? What is his net worth now? In 2021, *approximately $102 billion.* He's a billionaire times one hundred, but that doesn't make any difference to his dog, a Labrador retriever named Spinee. The lab doesn't see an investment icon when he runs to his master; he just sees Warren, an older man that really cares for him. It's cool that his master is a billionaire, but it doesn't drive Spinee's devotion to his master.

On good days and bad days, Spinee's always there for Warren. Just as Spinee focuses not on the financial power of his master but on just loving him, how can we look beyond the power and wealth of God and just love Him as our Master?

It's also cool that God created the universe and owns it all. *The Earth is the Lord's and all it contains*, far exceeding the wealth of Warren Buffett. Our devotion to God need not focus on His sovereign power and wealth but on His endless love. We are not dogs, and He doesn't treat us such, but we are wired to be cared for by a loving Father, not a government program. He sends His love on us. It is written: *While we were yet sinners, Christ died for us!*

You want to know God's love? Raise a puppy for a while. You'll see acceptance and mercy. Prince always looks back to me thinking: Are you there? Are you there? Are you still there? God says, *I'll never leave you or forsake you. NOTHING can separate you from My love. Neither can death, nor life, nor angels, nor principalities, nor powers, nor things present, nor things to come, nor height, nor depth, nor any other creature.* That's a solid promise from the Lord! You can boldly declare: "The Lord is my helper. Whom should I fear? What can man do to me?"

These are realistic promises from God. We recite them, but we don't experience them. Let's start experiencing the Word of God (personally) in our life. *Oh, taste and see that the Lord is good.*

Once, a man decided to buy me lunch and pointed out the sushi at the restaurant we were at. He said, "They do it right here." I told him I didn't like sushi. He asked what I didn't like about it, and my only answer was: "I haven't had it, but I don't like it!" Of course, he replied: "If you haven't tried sushi, how do you know you don't like it?" Unless you taste God, you can't say God's not good. If you taste God, there's no other taste on the planet that's as good as God.

We don't have to wonder about His side of the love equation. It's our side of that equation we have to come to grips with—and I guess I was struggling in that area (my part of that equation) when God sent Prince into my life to show me how He wants me to be fixed on Him and constantly adore Him. Why? So I can both rest in Him and bear fruit for Him. That's a life that is abundant and free.

All God wants is that we put our eyes on Him—to look at Him, talk to Him, listen to Him, read about Him. Just slow down and listen. God is speaking to us twenty-four-hours a day, seven days a week. We just have to ask: *What are You really saying to me?* and *Why are You saying it?* It's amazing how good God is.

I DARE YOU to divorce from anything less than devoted puppy love for God.

> *To fall in love with God is the greatest romance; to seek him the greatest adventure; to find him the greatest human achievement.*
> **– St. Augustine of Hippo**

> *But my eyes are toward You, O GOD, my Lord; in you I seek refuge; leave me not defenseless!*
> **– Psalm 141:8**

May you love the Lord more than life itself.

15

MANASSEH MEME

TO FIND THE TESTIMONY of King Manasseh, just go to the book of Kings and the Chronicles in the Old Testament. Remember who wrote the book. The priests were God's representatives on Earth (before God), and the prophets were God's representatives on Earth (representing God to man). Let's start there.

That's important to delineate.

Manasseh was twelve years old when he became king and reigned fifty-five years, so he was sixty-seven years old when he died. That's a long time to be king. So you've got to think about this. His father was King Hezekiah, a man of God.

When Manasseh became king at twelve, *who was running the kingdom?* He wasn't! He had counselors around him who were telling him what to do, right? But he was responsible. In time, he rebuilt the high places (pagan worship centers), which Hezekiah, his father, had broken down. He made altars for the Baals, he worshiped all the hosts of Heaven, and so on. A twelve-year-old can't make all those big decisions, so he had people around him that were coaching him in an evil, contemptible direction—much like in the USA currently.

Later in life, Manasseh made his children pass through the fire, desecrated the temple, blah, blah, blah. He did more evil than the nations around them that the Lord had destroyed! The Lord spoke, but Manasseh wouldn't obey.

Therefore, the Lord brought on the Assyrians, who took Manasseh and placed a nose hook on him (which I think was pretty cool). Once a nose hook's in place, all you need is a little pressure to gain total compliance. It's like a huge elephant being kept in place by a two-foot stake. It's hilarious. A little child could pull the stake out of the ground, but the elephant has been trained since birth that he can't move away from that stake. It's the same way when you get a nose hook on you . . . children pull you through the streets. This guy was humiliated. It was one of the worst humiliations you can think of, that he was being led by a nose hook; plus he had fetters around his ankles and his hands, and they pulled him about the streets naked.

"When he was in affliction, he . . . humbled himself greatly" (2 Chronicles 33:12, KJV). Manasseh prayed;

God received his prayer, heard his supplication, and brought him back to Jerusalem into his kingdom. "Then Manasseh knew that the Lord was God. Afterward he built an outer wall for the city of David . . . took away the foreign gods and the idol from the house of the Lord, and the altars that he had built . . . and he threw them out of the city. He also restored the altar of the Lord and . . . commanded Judah to serve the Lord" (2 Chronicles 33:13–16).

The key to it is he humbled himself. He went low. There are two paths to humility. (1) We get humbled when we encounter God's Word and see how far from His way we have strayed. Mostly, that straying emanates from what we willfully do, but sometimes it happens out of sheer ignorance. (2) Life events (we call circumstances) occur that we can't control.

Circumstances will humble you or harden you. Pharoah was briefly humbled, but at the end of the day, he was hardened. He said: *I'm not losing. No way!* He was humbled by God through Moses, but he would not stay low and look to God. He looked to himself and not to God. As a result, God took Pharoah's slaves away, and all the firstborn Egyptians died (including Pharoah's only son).

Let's do a comparison between the humiliation of Pharoah (which made him harder) and Nebuchadnezzar. Both guys were kings that are mentioned in the Scripture. The former got to stay in his palace and, in that comfort, hardened his heart against God and His people. Nebuchadnezzar, on the other hand, was removed from his kingdom, and his heart was turned to God as he was in the fields eating grass (like livestock) with dew on his back!

Circumstances will make you harder, or they will make you softer and able to repent before the Lord. There's no other way out. One of those two things will happen. When humility comes on you, you go right or you go left. Right is right—it's repenting. Starting with the point that Manasseh repented, it was a demonstration of the sorrow for what he did. He spent the rest of his life undoing decades of the evil things he had done, and he brought the people back to the Lord.

God gave him a do-over. He *got rid of the foreign gods, repaired the altar of the Lord, sacrificed peace offerings, and commanded Judah to serve the Lord. Nevertheless they still sacrificed in high places, but only to the Lord.* In other words, they didn't go to the temple in Jerusalem but sacrificed to God locally.

Manasseh had a passion to pull all that off, and I think that's huge! He was humbled and went the right way. He repented by changing his antipathy for God to gratefulness and a passion to honor God in all that he did. Nebuchadnezzar was humbled. Manasseh did the same things as Nebuchadnezzar, who said: *This is God.* Manasseh also realized *God is the Lord. He's the Only One.* God received his entreaty. Before Manasseh was humbled, all his sins, his trespasses, and the sites where he had built high places (set up wooden images and carved images) stood as monuments to Manasseh's evil heart. He's going: *OK, Lord, I'm wrong. You're God.* That prayer must have been AMAZING because God heard him. That's the key: God heard him, and He will hear us!

As mentioned earlier, a four-ton elephant can be paralyzed by a little stake in the ground because of conditioning. Manasseh was conditioned by others to make bad decisions, and then, later in life, he had to undo those decisions. What would it be like if we never had to undo the decisions that we made?

You can't talk your way out of what you behaved your way into. When we behave our way into something, we have to behave our way out, which requires humility and change (and that hurts), but that's our catalyst!

Let's go inward for a moment, OK?

Looking at these men and these examples, what can we personally learn in our own life, in our family, with our business?

What's on the table that we don't see?

What stake are we tied to that is holding us down? In other words, what stake (do we believe) is holding us back when it (in reality) doesn't have the power or authority to hold us back?

We may try to judge Manasseh and say: *Too little, too late.* Really? How about: *Better late than never?* The Manasseh meme is *Exhibit A* that it is never too late. *Never.* The repentant thief (on a cross next to Jesus) is *Exhibit B.* Don't miss the life lesson of these two men. In society, they were polar opposites: a wealthy king versus a poor thief. Yet God loved them both to the point of forgiveness. When God said He's no respecter of persons, He meant it. Whether you're a biker or a banker, His arms are open to your plea for forgiveness and desire to get right with Him.

God seeks a contrite heart, one that is truly sorry for messing up in life. He says: "Draw near to God, and he will draw near to you" (James 4:8). It's our *come-to-Daddy* moment. Why wait? It's never too late.

Come to Him with a heavy or contrite heart and a desire to know Him and be known by Him.

I DARE YOU to divorce from putting off your need for a Savior. It's not too late. You're not too dirty. Trust me, I know. Come to His open arms. They were open for me, and they are open for you.

Humility is not thinking less of yourself, it's thinking of yourself less.
– C. S. Lewis

Let us draw near with a true heart in full assurance of faith, with our hearts sprinkled clean from an evil conscience and our bodies washed with pure water.
– Hebrews 10:22

May you not be stuck seeing you as the world sees you. **May you** see in you what God sees in you, a redeemed person that needs an eternal loving Father.

Part III

ADDING THE PAINT

16

WHAT'S ESSENTIAL?

WHAT GOD IS TELLING ME during this novel coronavirus pandemic is: *Mike, it's not what you believe about Me; it's what you believe I believe about you. It's not what you think about Me; it's what you think I think about you.* (Wrap your mind around that, and it will transform your life.) God continues: *People think a lot of different things about Me. They have their own ideas and their own doctrines and idiosyncrasies, based on how they were raised and their background, and they think a lot of things about Me. But when you start to believe (after you understand) what I think about you, that's when your life will change.*

Don't dwell on the lens you have for Me. Instead, take the lens I have for you, and when you look through My lens, you will see My vision is far better than 20/20. I don't need glasses. I don't need eye drops. I can see clearly. And when I say to you, "This is what I see, this is who you are," I won't change my mind because this is the way I made you.

You have to remember, before I created you, before you were born from your mother's womb, I knew who you were going to be. I saw every decision and every choice you would make from the beginning of your life till the end of your life. I saw all the things you thought were good (that I didn't think were good). I saw things where you thought, "Oh this is bad," but those were good. You don't have to understand the way I view you.

Here's the most important thing: when you start understanding Me, you get your religious mindset out of the way, along with all your rules and regulations. When you approach Me with a filter based on regulations and law (and that's the way you are seeing Me), then that's the way you're going to think I look at you . . . and I don't. So, you need to drop your filter, burn it, throw it away, and realize what I see when I see you, what I think about when I think about you, and what I feel about you.

That is (straight-up) based on the cross.

Prior to your accepting Jesus as your Savior and Lord, I loved you. Do you hear Me? I loved you. No one could ever love you like I love you. My love will never end . . . ever. It doesn't change. The Law comes into play because the Law is meant to bring you to an understanding of why My Son came down to planet Earth, *was crucified, buried, and raised from the dead to return to Me.*

After that, you didn't need the Law because it was to lead you to a saving knowledge of Christ, so We could fill you with Our Spirit. Once Our Spirit is in you, then everything is based on love and faith. Therefore the Law is no longer directing you. The Spirit of God is directing you.

That's what God taught me through this quarantine. Here's what else: the United States and most state governments have deemed the church "non-essential." Governments throughout most communities say it's non-essential. This "business franchise" is not essential. What's interesting is that we (as a society) finally have seen what the Millennials have seen for decades . . . and they're right. The church, the institution, the building is NON-ESSENTIAL.

In Dallas, I go to a church building, and there are three thousand people, maybe more. Let's say I don't know anybody, and I don't want to know anybody, so I go sit down.

A man and his wife come up and sit down, and he asks, "How are you today?"

I say, "Great. How are you?"

"Fine."

"How's your wife?"

"Oh, she's doing great."

"Your kids?"

"Oh, they're great; everybody's great."

"OK," I say. All the while, they're not realizing that maybe I'm thinking about committing suicide. They'd never know that because I'm doing great.

On his part, he may be thinking about divorcing his wife, but he's not sharing that with me (or anybody else). He's just saying everything's great.

Basically what we're saying is hello (in a roundabout, pseudo-caring way). It's an elongated greeting. I acknowledge this human being sitting next to me, and I have to open my mouth because somebody's there. Then somebody else comes up and says, "Hey, how are you all doing?"

We tell him we're doing great, and we say to him, "Well, how are you doing?"

He goes, "I'm not doing too good, man. I'm really struggling over a lot of things."

We look at him and we go, "Uh . . . um . . . er . . . really? . . . Um, listen, we didn't ask you that. When we asked how you were doing, we just meant hello—don't go beyond that. We don't care what you're struggling with; we're not interested in what's going on inside you and your life." (Not everybody thinks this way, but most do.)

So that guy walks away.

Later, I get in my car, and some guy cuts me off. I roll my window down and tell that guy that I'm going to make his mother childless if he ever does anything like that again.

If those exchanges (at all) mirror our thoughts and actions, then the church is not essential, but I'll tell you what is essential.

What is essential is when Jesus is approached by a woman at the well in Samaria. Remember her in chapter 9, "Extracting the Precious from the Vile"? For us to encounter that woman and the realness of that woman is essential. It's essential that we meet in our homes and we open up our hearts and talk to each other about what we're struggling with. Not so we can change behavior, but so we can understand how God thinks about us and how He views us—what He has, His purposes and His plans for our life. THAT is essential.

What's not essential is the way we're doing church today in most (not all) churches. If a church comes through this Covid-19 the same way it was before, its members have learned nothing. They were given a chance for a do-over and completely dropped the ball. When Jesus forgave us and we confessed that Jesus is the Lord, God (at that moment) was ALL IN. He wasn't partially in; He wasn't thinking, *Let Me see before I make a full commitment.* God was all in. Here's what *all in* meant:

At that moment, He took away all my sin: past, present, and future. At that moment, He took it all away.

He put His Holy Spirit in me. If that wasn't enough, God also said He'd never leave me and He'd never forsake me, and He gave me promises I would never have to doubt about, for the rest of my life, because I would never, ever be able to understand how many there are. That's what He did *Day One*.

Every day after that is more simple than complicated. Get up, die to self, love God with all my heart, and love my neighbor as myself. Done! Everyday. Rinse and repeat. Yes, there's prayer in there and reading God's Word and meditating on it and doing good works, but those are tools to bear fruit. The most important things are faith *in God* and obedience *to God*.

I DARE YOU to divorce from majoring in the minors, from making mountains out of your various molehills. Grasp what is essential for your eternity and live in the present with that eternal perspective in mind!

> Choose to view life through God's eyes. This will not be easy because it doesn't come naturally to us. We cannot do this on our own. We have to allow God to elevate our vantage point. Start by reading

His Word, the Bible . . . Pray and ask God to transform your thinking. Let Him do what you cannot. Ask Him to give you an eternal, divine perspective.
– **Pastor Charles R. Swindoll**

He has told you . . . what is good; and what does the Lord require of you but to do justice, and to love kindness, and to walk humbly with your God?
– **Micah 6:8**

May you divorce from the non-essential things that distract you from an essential relationship with the Father by loving the Son and the people He loves.

17

THE CROSS MATTERS

IN A TIME WHEN hardly a news day goes by without a story about Black Lives Matter, we are beginning to see all comers exerting their people group as one that matters: Latino Lives Matter, Asian Lives Matter, Blue Lives Matter, and so on.

The obvious question is: Matters to whom? Me? You? The news media? The American justice system? Society as a whole? God?

We don't have to ask about God because He already declared who matters in John 3:16: "For God so loved the world." To God, the world matters. You, me, North Americans, South Americans, Africans, Europeans, and Asians. He is a global God. In fact, He is the God of the universe! God created the human race, so He looks at us as only one race! Would that we could be more like Him, but we want to feel we're the best and other people are either inferior or not as likable for some reason.

For instance, you may have heard the saying: "There are two kinds of people— Italians and those who wish they were." That is a soft form of Italian exceptionalism. Remember, it was hard-core German exceptionalism that caused WWII. Americans really don't care to be lumped in with Canadians, and Mexicans may not care to be lumped in with either Americans or Canadians! Same goes for Germans to Britons, to the French, and to Italians.

Yeah, we have unique differences, but if we go down the road of focusing on the differences—looks, food, language, culture—and do not consider our lives are but a vapor and we're gone (in the grand scheme of eternity), then we have short-sheeted the bed of life. Let's look at Latino Lives Matter. When you break Latino down, a Puerto Rican will say: "Well, I'm not from Colombia, and I'm not South American; I'm Puerto Rican. Don't call me Latino. Don't put me in that group!" You have Colombians, you have Argentinians, you have Ecuadorians, you have Peruvians, you have people from Brazil; they're all different. They're all different, but they're all Latinx because we group them as Latino. They, justifiably, say: "I'm not a Mexican; don't put me in that group." Same with Asians: "I'm not Japanese; I'm Chinese. Don't put me at group." "Hey, I'm Korean. Do not mix me up with a Taiwanese." But we consider them all Asian.

Demographically, we box people a big group, like Asian. Where's the box on the job application for your group? It doesn't have Taiwan, Chinese, Japanese, Malaysian, Burmese, or Vietnamese. It doesn't say any of that. It just says Asian. So you end up putting yourself in that box because that's what we have done. *We put people in boxes.*

The same way with the Middle East. "Man, I'm from Dubai, and I'm not from Bahrain, I'm not from Chad, I'm not from Syria, I'm not a Jew. I'm an Arab." We just put people in a box called Middle Eastern. *Come on, man.* What we're doing is boxing people in.

We talk about Black Lives Matter, Blue Lives Matter, Latino Lives Matter, You-Name-It Lives Matter.

Society wants to rank us according to color and culture, but here's what the apostle John said: "*For God so loved the world.*" He loved *the world.* That's the only box we check on His application.

God says: *I love everybody.* He gave His only Son that "whoever believes in him should not perish but have eternal life" (John 3:16). You know what? If we want to reduce Black Lives Matter, Blue Lives Matter, White Lives Matter, Brown Lives Matter, Latino Lives Matter, Asian Lives Matter, here's how we narrow it all down: **The Cross Matters**. That is the level playing field. The Cross Matters for all humanity. When the Cross Matters, then nothing else really matters.

All lives are the same in the eyes of God, but amongst people, we want to narrow this down into categories. We have A, B, C, D, E. We go to school. We get graded on a curve. We want to make sure everybody has a fair chance. You're an A student, but maybe I'm a C student, so they'd say: "I'm sorry. We checked your IQ out, and your IQ's not as high as this guy's." Then we get emotional quotients and personality profiles. We measure; we compare against other people. Why? Because we don't know any better. But God said: *You're all the same in My eyes.*

Imagine we are all standing on the California shore at Santa Monica. We're on the beach, and we're all going to participate in a swimming contest. I'm there, and so are sun-tanned older people (that swim all the time), young people, and folks in-between who want to swim. Then along comes Michael Phelps, the greatest swimmer in the world.

We're all about to jump in, and we ask: "Oh, by the way, what's the prize and where's the goal? What are we doing?"

The contest official says: "Oh, I'm sorry. I forgot to tell you that you're all going to swim to Hawaii."

The gun goes off, we all dive in and swim, but nobody makes it. Nobody. Michael Phelps gets farther than all of us. He gets ten miles, but it's 2,465 miles to

Hawaii! Everybody dies. I die, but even Michael Phelps dies. Nobody can make it. It's too great a distance.

The real goal is Heaven. How do we spend eternity with God? How do we do that? Is there an eternity? Is what we do in our life on planet Earth all there is? Is that it?

We don't remember being born. We don't know when we're going to die. We didn't have a choice in the color of our hair or the color of our skin. We didn't have a choice on how tall we would be, who are parents would be, or what country we would be born in. We had no vote in anything.

God didn't stop and say: *Excuse Me, I have about three seconds. I need you to make a quick decision while you're in the womb. Where do you want to be born? Want to be born in Germany? You don't?*

Shoot . . . OK. He doesn't want to be born in Germany. Let's make sure he's born in Spain. God didn't ask us anything. We're born. Here we are. We're alive on planet Earth, and now what? We think we control things? We think we have any say-so in anything?

God put an intellect in us to be able to choose and not choose. You take that intellect out of us, and we'd run back to God in a New York minute. We wouldn't have any choice, like a dog running to its owner. God loves *everyone*. God so loved Black Lives Matter, Blue

Lives Matter; God so loved the world—everybody: Muslims, Buddhists, Taoists, Shintos, Earth worshipers, Atheists, Agnostics, even satanists! (Side note: Isn't it interesting that Muslims call Abraham their father, Jews call Abraham their father, and Christians call Abraham their father? We have the same father, right? What happens when it comes down to Jesus?)

I love what Psalm 139:14 says: "I am fearfully and wonderfully made." What does that mean? That means that if all humans are wonderfully made, then all skin color (as diverse as it is) is wonderful to God!

Ever think about that?

At the end of the day, what matters in life, the entire reason we—every human being, every soul, every man, woman, and child—are alive today on planet Earth is for one reason: *to love and serve our Creator*. In studying history and civilizations, there's only one piece of history that matters: it's the cross. The Cross Matters.

As the seventies song says, "We are the world." There's no planet like us. It's OK to have borders. It's OK to have national sovereignty. Those are privileges we can use for good or for harm. God would like us to see people as He sees them.

Here's how we typically see people: As soon as we lay eyes on them, our brain takes in data: clothing, height, weight, eyes, teeth, hair, facial hair, voice, accent, mannerisms, and so on. Sadly, those inputs are processed to find not what there is to love but what there is to react to . . . or at least be skeptical of.

Here's how God sees a person: ♥

He sees you as lovely. He sees you as being made in His image. He sees you as precious. He sees you as a rare and valuable pearl (worth selling everything to buy). How do I know this? Because His Word reveals that to us in Matthew 13:45–46: "The kingdom of heaven is like a merchant in search of for fine pearls, who, on finding one pearl of great value, went and sold all that he had and bought it."

Who was the merchant? *Jesus was.* What was the price He paid for us? *His mortal body, His human life.* He gave it ALL for us because He was all-in from the beginning.

He didn't commit suicide. No, He was not like that. That would have been too easy and would not have fulfilled the prophecies about Him and His suffering for you and me. The much harder road was, in essence, a Roman road, specifically a Roman cross. What's the big deal about a Roman crucifixion?

Buckle up your seatbelts and I'll tell you.

Even though God loves us, there is a huge thing that keeps us from a relationship with Him. Adam and Eve had a glorious relationship with Father God. They got to enjoy Eden together in the cool of the evening.

Ahhh, what a blessed and amazing privilege they had. Until . . . the fallen angel came one day and tricked Eve into disobeying God and eating from the one tree they were forbidden to partake of.

He twisted what God had warned them about, and she bought his scam. Afterwards, her husband ate also, and they went from Heaven-sent to Hell-bent creatures. When God came for the daily stroll, they hid themselves from Him because they experienced a new emotion, shame, and a new feeling, guilt. *They had never had either before!* God knew. He confronted them, and in His mercy, He chose to banish them from the Garden of Eden, rather than kill them on the spot.

Though many generations removed, we are all of the seed of Adam through Noah. God, in His sovereignty, created humans to have a free will. We are free to love Him, and we are free to hate or ignore Him, but we are never out of His attention, His reach, and His care.

Mankind broke a holy relationship with the God of the universe, and there was no way for man to fix it.

Adam and Eve had two sons. In adulthood, one brother killed the other in a fit of jealousy. Ever since then and, of course, to this day, people kill and hurt other people. In my hometown of Chicago, a person is murdered every ten hours! That's 2.4 murders a day 365 days a year!

In time, God's people became slaves of the Egyptian empire for a while. Like . . . four hundred years. On July 4, 2021, America turned 245 years old. Now consider what four hundred years of slavery must have been like. The evil Atlantic African slave trade to the Americas lasted from 1650 to 1900; that's 250 years. Don't get me wrong; 250 *hours* of slavery is wrong and evil. I view slavery as one barometer of the depravity of man's heart. I'm just saying the Jews definitely had their share (about thirteen generations). Later, God took the Hebrews out of slavery and out of Egypt to head to the land promised centuries before to Abraham. They rebelled, and only the young people were allowed in with their two remnant elders: Joshua and Caleb.

Later, they were given judges to keep their moral compass God-ward, but the people rebelled and insisted they have kings like other nations. Out of forty-one kings, thirty-three were bad and did the people harm by estranging them from the God of their fathers and following other gods. Eventually, the rule of the kings of Israel and Judah ceased, and the Romans occupied the land, including Jerusalem, by conquest.

During this time, a favored Hebrew virgin, named Mary, conceived a holy child and called Him Jesus (Yeshua, to be exact). When the iron fist of Rome threatened the boy's life, his parents fled to Egypt as refugees. When God took out their Roman persecutor, they were free to return to their homeland. That is where Jesus grew up, in the town of Galilee. (Born in Bethlehem, raised in Galilee).

He lived a sinless life. Not a life without temptations of pride, greed, lust, and the like. He experienced all those. It is not a sin to be tempted. The sin comes when we act on those temptations. It was a main reason the Son of God came to the Earth as the Son of Man—to face all that men have to face and so we *would have a High Priest who was tempted in all ways as we are, yet without sin.*

At age thirty, Jesus entered the waters of the Jordan River, where his cousin John (the baptizer) was baptizing. For everyone else, John's baptism was a baptism of repentance, but for Jesus, it was a baptism of the Holy Spirit.

Right after that, Jesus fasted for forty days and forty nights, whereupon satan sought opportunity to tempt Him in grander ways than he tempts us. Once, twice, three times. With every punch of the enemy, Jesus landed a stronger counter-punch: *It is written . . . It is written . . . It is written* (quoting the Torah), till the devil had enough and left. It was a fight. Not MMA, but no less a real battle of opposing forces. In the end, starved of water and food, Jesus KO'd satan in the third round. Immediately afterwards, the angels were in His corner.

That began a three-year ministry to the "lost sheep of the house of Israel," where He healed the brokenhearted and caused the deaf to hear, the lame to walk, the blind to see, as well as performed many other signs and wonders, including raising a man, a girl, and a woman from the dead on three different occasions. The man was Lazarus. He had been dead four days (in his tomb) when Jesus commanded him to come out of it. He walked out—looking like a live mummy because his burial linens were still on him! That one miracle led many to Christ.

You'd think that the arrival of the Messiah would be met with overwhelming joy and hope from the Jewish religious leaders of the day. It was just the opposite! They hated Him. As Jesus went about doing what He was doing, they looked like weak, powerless, prideful, yet fearful men. As a point of fact, they were.

Jesus became the center of attention when *they* preferred to be the center of attention. Jesus took the promise of eternal life with the Father to their turf: Jerusalem and other cities. As time went on, even more sought Jesus. He fed five thousand men (and their families) in the wilderness, He preached with authority, He was God incarnate, and those jealous leaders were merely sons of their father, the father of lies.

They had to think of a way to cancel Jesus, get Him out of their town and out of their lives. One day, they got a break. Judas Iscariot, one of the twelve men of Jesus's inner circle, showed up during the feast of Passover to betray Jesus into their hands. The members of the Sanhedrin and the scribes were thrilled and even paid Judas thirty pieces of silver for his trouble.

Having (long ago) foretold His disciples how this would end, Jesus took eleven of them to the Garden of Gethsemane to pray before the storm of religious vengeance came to take Him. After healing one of the temple servants of his severed ear, Jesus willingly let the guards escort Him to the father of the high priest. Later He was interrogated by the high priest in the middle of the night under cover of darkness. The exchange had all the markings of a vigilante trial.

Satisfied that Jesus should be condemned to death, the high priest had no authority in the Torah to do so.

Thus, they turned Jesus over to the Roman civil authority, Pontius Pilate, governor of the region.

This paragon of political appointees had Jesus scourged with a Roman cat-o-nine-tails. It was a whip with nine leather straps attached to a wood handle.

Embedded in the end of the straps were either shards of glass or razor-sharp chunks of metal.

When the Roman torturer flogged Jesus with the whip, the brunt of the leather tore into His back, but the tips wrapped around His side as the sharp objects took hold. If you can imagine, as I can, that the Roman tormenter had forearms the size of most men's thighs, then you understand how he used his strength to scrape those objects across Jesus's ribcage to the side of his back. Over and over and over again and again. Words cannot fully describe the pain inflicted by the sickening process of utter humiliation and torture. Lesser men die on the spot.

Later, the Roman soldiers sat Him in a chair, blindfolded Him, and punched Him in the face. They sneered: *Prophesy who punched You!* Jesus turned the cheek many times till He was beaten beyond recognition. They weren't seeking a confession from Jesus. They wanted to exact Roman terror on a man Pilate snidely labeled as the "King of the Jews." Friends, this is just the prelude of what's to come. The time came for the execution of Pilate's death sentence upon Jesus and two convicted thieves. They were all led out of Jerusalem to a hill nicknamed The Skull. Part of the humiliation show was to have each prisoner carry the large wooded crossmember, from which they would soon hang. Jesus, though hideous to look at, carried His cross as far as He was humanly able. Finally, His body could not take another step, and He fell to the ground.

Because His welts and open, bleeding sores on His back were so evident, the soldiers thought it pointless to whip Him into getting up and proceeding. Instead, they ordered a Black bystander (from Cyrene, a suburb of Ethiopia) to carry the crossmember for Him.

At the foot of the hill, the crossmembers were set horizontally. Jesus was laid on top of the wood with one arm stretched to His right and the other to His left. With sharp blows, the soldier drove a spike in the first wrist (between the bones). Can you spell P-U-R-E A-G-O-N-Y? Then the other wrist also had a stake, or large nail, driven through it to the wood beneath.

More unadulterated agony. Then, Jesus was raised upon the "tree," His feet were crossed over each other, and one more spike was driven through both feet. The horrible day got even worse. Now, He was vertical and bleeding and put on display.

The Romans knew that public death sentences are a very effective deterrent to unwanted societal behavior. They expected it would be generations before any Hebrew would rise up and contend to be the King of the Jews after this crucifixion.

The guilty ones on either side of Him said what everyone was thinking: *If You are who You say You are, then get off your stinkin' cross. Oh, and by the way, take us off with You!* (I am totally paraphrasing here).

The sad part was He could have gotten off, but that would have been at our expense. Remember, I said mankind could not fix the separation from God that began with Earth's first couple. So it had to come down to this—not just death but the cruelest, bloodiest Roman death of the most innocent of innocents. Jesus was, and is, the Lamb of God who was sacrificed for your sins, transgressions, and iniquities—as well as mine!

THIS is why the Cross, and only the Cross, Matters. Without it, we'd all be dead in our sins and have zero hope of entering into the loving presence of the Father. *The only color that mattered that day was red . . . His blood.* Since the days of ceremonial Temple sacrifices, remission of sin comes only by blood. There is no other means of accomplishing redemption.

If there were any other way, Jesus would not have had to endure our sufferings on His body and shed His blood for our sins. All because God gave us the choice to be holy or unholy. The world *matters* to God, Jesus *matters* to us, so the cross *matters* to everyone!

I DARE YOU to divorce from a life of *self* and any thoughts that would place you below or exult you above people of any skin color. Fully consider the cross of Jesus. Be laser-focused on His cross, and then take Him up on the blood covenant, which redeemed us (bought us back) from sin as our master. Before we were even born, He loved us. So now *we love Him because He first loved us and gave Himself for us!*

The next key to being full-on with Jesus is to die to ourselves. He wants us to follow His footsteps and take up our cross daily. Die to self; live for Him and in Him. There's no better way to live.

> Before we can begin to see the cross as something done for us, we have to see it as something done by us.
> **– John Stott**, theologian

> *Looking to Jesus, the founder and perfecter of our faith, who for the joy that was set before him endured the cross, despising the shame, and is seated at the right hand of the throne of God.*
> **– Hebrews 12:2**

May the cross of Christ be your all in all. We are nothing without it, but we are everything with it!

18

CANCEL CULTURE BEGAN IN THE CHURCH

WOULD THAT THIS WERE NOT TRUE, but it is.

For decades, the "good people" of our country's churches looked down on others. I know. *I was one of them.* We had a rubber stamp that spelled **CANCEL.** Whenever we were confronted by "those people," we whipped out our stamp and *Bam!* They were canceled—canceled from attending services or not invited to meetings and Bible studies, canceled from sharing a meal together, canceled from being loved and cared for. Some of this canceling was enshrined in governmental policies, but most of it emanated from our churches, you know, those places that preach about Jesus—that guy who was a friend of sinners. By the 2020 US election, the folks that we (and Hillary Clinton) might call "deplorables" had mounted an all-out offensive on American culture and politics. When the dust settled in January of 2021, the reins of power were switched. and now *they* were holding the CANCEL rubber stamp. Swiftly, they began to apply it to everyone that ever dismissed or canceled them: politicians, preachers, teachers, administrators, police officers, women in sports (that insist on only competing against other women), statues of famous Americans, you name it. Even *Harry Potter* author J. K. Rowling and Dr. Suess were victims of their animus!

The problem isn't that they were obsessing with the CANCEL stamp; the problem is that such a stamp was in our hands (to begin with) before being pried from our fingers by political force. *We* held a stamp that they could steal and use against us. Guess what? They did, and *it's payback time!*

Specifically, what has religion done? We canceled the people that were saying (back in the day): "I'm a homosexual. You put me down for it, and I don't believe I can help it." That's what we have done, as a church, to countless people. We cast them out of our private, religious society, and from that, we stamped a not-so-subtle inference: *You are worthless; you mean nothing*, and we canceled them out. We put them in a box by themselves. That left us feeling safe and secure in our world.

There are churches in Dallas whose doors are open for people that are gay, lesbian, and so on. They're welcome there. They preach Jesus, and they preach Jesus crucified, buried, and resurrected. They exist for that group of people that feel the church won't let them into our doors because we don't know how to deal with such a group (in love). We don't know how to say: "What you're doing offends God," without being angry. We don't know how to speak the truth in love. When we do speak the truth, we're pissed off and angry. That means we're going to put them down, and we're going to condemn them (the very thing God doesn't do) because they can't, or won't, refuse to change their behavior.

Absent hearts of love, we were as apostle Paul described, "noisy cymbals and clanging brass." So the subculture put up with that for decades, and then it went to the lesbians, and then it went to the transvestites, and now it's LGBTQIAQ+! *What does that even mean?* They're just adding more and more and more. Now *they* say: "*We're* canceling *you* out. *We* finally have a voice. *We* have finally risen up against you and your loveless beliefs."

Friends, we are eating the fruit of the seeds we planted in our life. This bears repeating: *We, as the church, are eating the fruit of the seeds we planted.* As the Word says, we are reaping what we sowed. When is the best time to plant a tree? Today? No, today is a good time, but it's not the best time. *Ten years ago* was the best time to plant a tree because we're eating of its fruit today. The next best time is today, because we're going to (in the future) look back and be glad we planted that seed.

So we are eating the fruit of the seeds we planted (as a community) because we've neglected this group of people (that we didn't want anything to do with). The silent majority are us—you and me—because we allowed the church to do that. We may say: "Well, you know, we were speaking the truth." Of course, we couldn't stand against the truth, but we could have stood up against *the heartless way* the truth was presented.

That's why the Millennials today (even Generation Z) are reacting to organized religion. They're not fighting the truth. They're fighting the way the truth is presented. That's why they've left churches in droves. They're fed up with the BS mega-churches where the pastors are driving around in Bentleys.

They just can't get their mind wrapped around that. They don't understand it, like: *Why is it OK for you guys to talk bad about everything, yet you live a completely different lifestyle?* That's why nobody could say anything against Mother Teresa because she walked the truth. She walked the truth because she walked the talk. It was more than her message; it was the selfless way she lived her life.

I once heard a saying that made me think: "Preach the gospel every day. If necessary, use words." We're not preaching the gospel with our lifestyle, with what we walk out with our feet. We're wordy. We're just a bunch of words walking around, feeling and knowing, suggesting: *Yeah, we did the right thing. We're doing the right thing. Yeah, everything's right.* But we're eating bitter fruit from our own seeds of the loveless, uncaring attitude we planted years ago.

I've got to look at my own life. We're planting seeds, and we're getting down on the fruit that we're eating. We're complaining about the fruit, but we are the ones that planted the seeds! We water them, and later, we don't like what's grown up. We should plant different seed today because, three years from now, it's going to be here, and by God's grace and mercy, we'll still be alive so we can start eating better fruit, not bitter fruit.

In the past, we planted some bamboo. When we come against the lesbian, gay, bisexual, trans-sexual, queer, and the other ones are: *I-don't-know-what-I-am-but-I- can-be-whatever-I-want-to-be*, we've come against that so hard because we planted bamboo shoots.

When you plant bamboo seeds in the ground, they go only about twelve inches deep, but their root system can go horizontally for football fields! Bamboo can grow through cracks in concrete! Bamboo is used (in China) as an active torture because it can grow through human flesh. It can grow through organs and grow through human bodies. That's what bamboo does over time. But planted in the earth, you can't see it because it's underground. When you try to pull bamboo out of your yard, it's difficult because there's a root system that's been there a long time.

That's what we've done, so let's be responsible. Let's take ownership of this mess we've made. I can't blame the institutional church. I can't blame the mega-churches. I've got to blame me. I can do my part, I can write books about it, I can talk about it, I can complain about it, I can judge other people that aren't like me, but that's not it. That's not walking out a life of love.

What am I doing *today* in my community? What am I doing next month besides praying and reading the Word? How am I walking out the cancel culture today? I planted the seeds for them to do what they're doing to me. I'm complaining against it, but what do we do? What are the next steps? It's got to start with me.

Number 1: Get alone with God and say: "Lord, I'm not part of the problem—I *am* the problem. I am the problem, and I'm sorry that I have not seen the bigger picture by seeing what You see. I've seen people going against what the Scriptures teach, and instead of learning to get close to them and love them, I judged them (from a distance) and I wanted nothing to do with them—which means I canceled them out of my life."

We cannot fail to be aware that this is exactly what we have done *personally*. Not other people, not another group, but I have done this. I've got to start there and think: *OK, now what's my next step after I've changed my mind and come into agreement with God (that I've not loved these people properly as God would do)? What is my next step from there when I, first of all, take responsibility?*

Now, I don't want to go to the total opposite side—where I just walk around and tolerate it. So, there's a middle ground, which is the true ground. As John 1:14 says: "the only Son from the Father, full of grace and truth." We're good at pushing truth, but we don't mix it with grace so that we live out the fragrance of both of them. To the world, we don't quite smell right. Jesus was full of truth. Jesus was full of grace. He was both. I want to be graceful, speaking the truth in love (with grace).

Many look at grace as toleration. They look at the truth in the Law, and they get angry if you're not doing the right thing. Then they say you're tolerating if you don't say anything about evil behavior. So, how do we walk that middle ground?

Number 2: Take responsibility. That means owning up to my past actions or feelings and repenting of my loveless, self-centered, gotta-be-like-the-Joneses attitude.

That doesn't mean I'm tolerant, but I have to start with me. *Lord, what do You say?* I know what Your Word says. I know what Your Law says and that Your Law has been fulfilled in me—who walks not according to the flesh but according to the spirit. The spirit of God, certainly, is not judging those people. No way the spirit of God is judging them; impossible. So what do I do after I get alone with God and realize I am the problem? I get God's mind towards it—which is mercy and grace and truth. Then, what do I do (after I've prayed)? How do I walk this out?

Number 3: Ask myself WHY? Why did I buy and wear the Cancel Culture T-shirt and look down on those who were not like me and not care? Now, I am not like *them*, and they don't care about *me*. What's my *why* behind the *what*? If we're honest, our answer will lead us to discover things like family biases, but that isn't personal enough. We can hide behind stuff like that. Why did Mike write these people off? (Be brutally honest.) If you can't think why, then pray it through: "Father, show me the real me. Show me the me that disappointed You over how I ignored Your mandate to love my neighbor."

Number 4: Figure out that anyone and everyone's your neighbor. Did I define *neighbor* so narrowly that it just happened to be only friends of mine? Who does God say my neighbor is?

What if God answers you in broad terms—*anyone who isn't a member of your immediate family*? Better yet how about: *anyone you share common oxygen with*. (That's everybody!) That crosses ages, genders, skin colors, religions, economic status, education, disabilities, languages, you name it! *That's* our neighbor.

Come to grips with the fact that Mister Rogers is dead and that folks need *you* to be their neighbor. *Please won't you be their neighbor?*

Number 5: Confess to God and to representatives of the people you used to look away from. Scripture gives us this promise: "If we confess our sins, he is faithful and just to forgive us our sins and to cleanse us from all unrighteousness" (1 John 1:9). Let's clear our conscience and make things right with the Lord. We know He'll forgive us.

Number 6: Reach out to those we love to hate (or look down upon). Yeah, that will be awkward, and everything in us will fight against going there because the enemy knows how effective it is to humble ourselves before others in meekness.

Let's say you have a gay neighbor next door. Can you owe it to God to stop by and say something like: "I know you are gay and you know I am not. We are different in that respect. But I am ashamed of how I have looked down on men and women like you [never say *you people*], and I've come to say I am sorry. I have let both you and God down with my wrong attitude towards gays and lesbians. I can't agree with it, but I want to stop looking down on people and start looking up to God. Please forgive me."

I DARE YOU to divorce *not* getting right with your neighbors, the ones who are not like you. I'm not asking you to be like them or become BFFs; just quit judging them and show them you care. Whether they forgive you, cry and hug you, or tell you to go to Hell, it needs to be done to unravel (to reverse) the Cancel Culture that affects us all. You are not responsible for their will, but you are responsible for your will.

> Judging others makes us blind, whereas love is illuminating.
> **– Dietrich Bonhoeffer**

If you are offering your gift at the altar and there remember your brother has something against you, leave your gift there before the altar and go. First be reconciled to [get right with] your brother, and then come and offer your gift [to the Lord].
– Matthew 5:23-24

May you have the courage to make things right before God and man. Do not give in to the fear of other people's responses. Un-cancel them, even if they continue to cancel you.

19

DEAD MAN WALKING

IN THE MADE-FOR-TV SERIES *Band of Brothers*, the soldiers are getting ready to fight. A trooper named Albert Blyth confides with the lieutenant about his D-Day landing experience and says: "I was scared." The lieutenant said: "We're all scared." He later tells private Blyth: "The only hope you have is to accept the fact that you are *already dead*. The sooner you accept that, the sooner you'll be able to function as a soldier is supposed to function . . .: without mercy, without remorse. All war depends upon it."

Every day that we get to breathe is a gift, and I think, when we wake up in the morning, we don't realize this, but we will benefit by that daily revelation.

Every day, when we wake up, here's the first thing we need to hear God say: *I determined whether you wake up. Not satan, not the enemy, but I decided that.* We woke up! Each of our days begins with a victory!

Instead of us complaining, the enemy (satan) should be saying—"Oh no . . . he's up again." If we're walking with the Lord, it's the enemy that should be freaked out! When believers walk into a room, satan and the demons are afraid of us. We carry around life! We carry with us the Spirit of the Most High God. He has already judged satan and his demonic minions. They haven't seen their end yet, but we've seen our end.

Our end is with God forever.

Our eternal life doesn't start when we die, it starts on planet Earth. *We're already dead.* We're dead men walking. Everything after that is a gift: clothing is a gift, homes are a gift, money's a gift, travel's a gift, food is a gift, wine is a gift.

When we place our gifts above the Gift-Giver we miss it. God owns it all. He says: *I have the ability to give you whatever you desire because I own the Earth and all it contains.* Why do we seek the gift and not the Giver? We are seeking God's hand, not His face, not His eyes, not His heart. Most of the time, we look at His hands—*what's He giving me today?*

Let's picture this in our minds each day: Think about a little child that wakes up and walks out of her room and the first person she sees is her dad, standing at the door. Her dad says, "Hey honey, I've hidden a gift in the house for you." She's gets all bright-eyed, and she's running around, looking underneath the couch and taking the pillows out, and there's a little gift hidden for her. She exclaims: "Oh, Daddy, I found it! Thank you, Daddy."

Then the next day, she gets up and goes to the door, and her dad is standing there. "Honey I got a gift." "Really, Daddy?" So she's running around looking for the gift, and she finds the gift. He does that the next day and . . . all week.

At what point does that child wake up in the morning and the first thing on her mind is "Daddy's waiting for me; he's got a gift"? She opens the door, and there's Daddy again. What if we woke up every day, as adults, with the same trust and anticipation?

The Lord says: *I have a gift for you. It's hidden in the day. Walk around with the life I put in you, and just wait and look for the blessing that I have for you.*

Look for it. It's in the day.

Maybe you bless somebody, maybe you help somebody out, maybe you pull your car over to help someone, maybe you give a few dollars to a beggar on the street—I don't know what it is, but God has the best planned for us every single day.

How do I know that? Because He said it in Jeremiah 29:11: "For I know the plans I have for you, declares the Lord, plans for welfare and not for evil, to give you a future and a hope." To paraphrase Isaiah 55:8–9: My thoughts are not your thoughts; My ways are not your ways. For as the heavens are high above the earth, so is the difference between. That is, there's a difference in way God thinks about you and thinks about the world versus the way you think about you and think about the world. Certainly, the way you think of other people is different from the way God thinks of people.

Most of us, upon arising, assume this is the way God must think about me. But God's saying: *No, My thoughts are not your thoughts, but if you could understand My thoughts, you'd know I love you without limit.*

To think like God, we have to change the way we think. When we change the way we think and we change the way we understand (how God views us, other people, and situations), that will change who we are. Paul says in Galatians 2:20: "I have been crucified with Christ. It is no longer I who live, but Christ who lives in me. And the life I now live in the flesh, I live by faith in the Son of God, who loved me and gave himself for me." He also said in 2 Corinthians 5:17: "If anyone is in Christ, he is a new creation. The old has passed away, the new has come."

We're already dead. If we're dead, everything we see and experience in life is a gift. It has to be because we're dead; we're not alive. If you take a dead man and put him up against a wall, and you take the most beautiful women in the world and parade them in front of this guy, it's impossible for him to lust because he's dead. He can't; he's dead!

Consider yourselves dead to sin but alive to God in Christ Jesus. Read Romans 6. We need to sit and consider, *Who am I?* We're dead men walking.

That's what they say when a prisoner is on death row. When taken out of his cell to go to the electric chair or injection site, what do the prison guards say as they're walking down the hall? They say: "Dead man walking, dead man walking, dead man walking." He's not dead; he's still alive, but they say he's dead because he's going to die.

The prisoners understand: *Here is a dead man walking because the death penalty's been decreed over him.* By the decree of the law, voiced by the prison warden, he's considered dead.

God made a decree over us: *you're dead to sin, but you're alive to Jesus.* That's a decree God made, so it's the truth. So we best walk that out.

Every day you wake up starts with a victory because getting up that morning means satan's desire to steal, kill, and destroy us (throughout the night) was prevented. It was defeated by God's providence and power.

There was a minister named John G. Lake who was a gifted healer in his day. He knew who he was (in Christ) and how to live that out. During his ministry, there was a plague, a serious pandemic (if you will), and he ministered to sick and dying people as if nothing was going to happen to him.

The reporters asked him, "Why aren't you getting sick? This is a most deadly virus!"

He said, "No, not me. I have God in me; this just can't touch God." To illustrate his point, he said, "Here, put it on my hand."

They put a live, deadly virus on his hand. Then they took it off his hand and put it under the microscope. It showed that every live virus had died as soon as it had touched him! He knew exactly who he was.

John G. Lake would go in the front doors of quarantined houses and pray for people. The cops and health authorities would wait for him at the street, but he'd go out the back door and off to the next home in need. At the height of his ministry (praying in faith) the town where he was headquartered (Spokane, Washington) had to close its hospital! That's a known fact.

What's so special about John G. Lake? Just one thing: he trusted God's power and promises as recorded in His Word. You and I have that same Word lying somewhere in our house or in a hotel room drawer.

Let's read it. Better yet, let's believe it and act on those beliefs!

I DARE YOU to divorce from living as though you were *not* dead. The sooner you accept that, the sooner you'll be able to function as a soldier of the Cross is supposed to function. All victory, in Christ, depends upon it.

> We cannot exercise our faith beyond what we believe to be possible.
> **– John G. Lake**

> *How precious to me are Your thoughts, O God! How vast is the sum of them!*
> *If I would count them, they are more than the sand. I awake, and I am still with you.*
> **– Psalm 139:17-18**

May you engrave God's Word in your mind and heart—to walk in unwavering faith and victory!

20

WANNA BE A LEADER? LEAD!

WE BECOME TRUE LEADERS when we understand that, to lead properly and to make decisions as leaders, we have to learn how to destroy our assumptions.

I heard a great challenge from a man named Doug Morrow. He told me this: "A man walks up to a woman and takes all her clothes off without touching her." Next, Doug says, "Ask me yes or no questions to discover what happened."

"Was she offended?"

"No."

"Did she appreciate what he did?"

"Not particularly."

"Was he right to do that?"

"No or Yes."

"Was he related to her?"

"Not important."

"Did he sin?"

"Not with her."

"Was he a doctor?"

"No."

See, it's our assumptions that cause us to hit walls and not process what really happened. A man walked up to a woman and took all her clothes off without touching her. ANSWER: He walked up to her wearing some of her clothes and he took them off.

In our brain, we assumed the woman was wearing the clothes that the man took off. We didn't realize he was wearing her clothing (over his own clothing perhaps). Our brains don't even try to go there because our assumptions won't let us!

We assumed she was wearing the clothes that were taken off. Those assumptions cause us to go down roads that mess us up when we lead others because we're on the wrong road to begin with. Here's another one . . .

A man wants to go home, but there's a man with a mask at home. Tell me what's going on from asking yes-or-no questions. Your investigation would go something like this:

Is the man with a mask a burglar?

No.

Is there a costume party going on?

No.

Is the man concerned about Covid-19?

No.

Is the man at home a baseball catcher in full gear? YES!

You're starting to break out of it. That's very good. Most people can't even get there. My point is our assumptions hinder us from being leaders.

We assume everybody's read the Bible. We assume this; we assume that. We assume *born again* means this, and we immediately assume if you are a believer, this is what your behavior looks like. These assumptions God does not put on us. He does not assume anything! (Because He knows everything.) He never had an opinion or a new thought.

"Hey, Father."

"Yeah, Jesus?"

"Hey, I was just thinking (such and such)."

Wow, never thought of that! No, even Jesus can't give God a new thought.

When we make assumptions about other people (not knowing factual information), we set ourselves up for bad judgment. When we look for something to support that assumption, we will find it. Then, when we find it, we will judge it or react to it or respond to it. It all starts with an assumption.

I DARE YOU to divorce from limiting assumptions. Broaden your thoughts and assumptions, while staying clear of delusions or bizarre conclusions. If you want to be a good leader, then "what if . . ." is a good question to ask yourself before making decisions.

Counsel in the heart of man is like deep water; but a man of understanding will draw it out.
– Proverbs 20:5 (KJV)

May you ask God for wisdom and discernment and apply both with integrity.

21

APOSTLE 13

MOST CHRISTIANS CANNOT NAME the twelve Hebrew patriarchs, the sons of Isaac (the son of Abraham). They might remember Joseph, who was sold by his half-brothers as a slave. He went from slave to prisoner and then to Pharoah's right-hand man, the second most powerful human in Egypt! But, hey, that's the Old Testament, right?

What about Jesus's twelve apostles, His inner circle? Can we name them? *Uhhh . . . Peter, James, John . . . hmm. What does it matter?* Well, we're told in the book of Revelation that the twelve foundations of the celestial city (named the New Jerusalem) will be of stone with these men's names on each layer. Seems kind of important to God.

I don't want to guilt-trip anybody, OK? But, for the record, here are their names:

1. Peter
2. James (son of Zebedee)
3. John
4. Philip
5. Bartholomew
6. Matthew
7. Thomas
8. James (son of Alpheus)
9. Simon
10. Jude (also called Thaddeus)
11. Andrew (and)
12. Matthias (replacing Judas Iscariot)

The question I put to you is this: *Who said Jesus could have only twelve apostles?*

First, we should make a distinction between *founding* apostles and *on-going*, or operational, apostles. The founding apostles had ALL been with Jesus at His baptism in the Jordan River, all the way till His Ascension back to glory. A man who was not with Jesus in all those places could not be a founding apostle. I'm not giving my opinion here; this is what Peter said as they were about to replace Judas Iscariot as the twelfth apostle. Beyond the first twelve, all other apostles just need to love God and be called by Him to serve in such a capacity. That means doing one or more of the following:

- Establish churches
- Equip saints
- Preach to and/or protect the church
- Identify and commission elders in their area
- Make decisions for the Body
- Oversee and/or counsel a city or region of churches

In Ephesians 4:11–12, the apostle Paul lays out what my friend Pastor Bill Johnson calls the five-fold ministries that Jesus gave the saints. "And He Himself gave some to be apostles, some prophets, some evangelists, and some pastors and teachers for the equipping of the saints for the work of the ministry, for the edifying of the body of Christ" (NKJV).

Wow! What do we have operating now? *Some* evangelists, *a lot of* pastors, and *even more* teachers. The MIAs in most churches are apostles and prophets, *the very first two that are mentioned!* How can that be a scriptural arrangement?

Let's say you are baking a cake that has five ingredients. You're in a hurry, and you use only three of the five ingredients. *How's that cake going to turn out?* Would you serve that cake to God? *Of course not!* Yet that is exactly what churches around the world are serving God: incomplete (and likely inedible) cakes.

By ignoring the recipe Jesus gave us, we end up with cakes (ministries, programs, events, worship times) that are lacking and deficient. We expect God to be pleased at being served a flat cake, with no baking powder and salt in it! In other words, no apostle or prophet.

I would like to expand our thinking as to what an apostle is by introducing a person we'll nominate to be the thirteenth apostle. Nowhere in Scripture will you see that title conferred on this person, but this person lived it out. Living it out is always better than sitting around with a badge. As the true saying goes: "Well done is better than well said."

One day, Jesus and His disciples were going through Samaria. He sent them on an errand, so He was alone when He came to a well. We looked at the woman He met there in chapter 9, "Extracting the Precious from the Vile," so I won't repeat the talk between her and Jesus.

The point is this. By Jesus caring for her, prophesying, and teaching her, she was (by His actions and her response) equipped and *sent out* to tell others. She ran to her city and informed all the men about the man who "told me everything I ever did." I called her a one-minute missionary in that previous chapter.

Was this woman the thirteenth apostle (because she encountered Jesus long before Saul of Tarsus, renamed Paul)? If she is not an apostle, then where does she fit in the five-fold ministry (if at all)? How about Junia? Is she the thirteenth apostle? She is called an apostle by Paul in Romans 16:7, along with Andronicus. Let's just emphasize that it is Jesus, not the church, who makes apostles. The church is asked to make *disciples* (other followers of The Way). To those who were taught there are only twelve apostles, where do we see Paul saying that he is an apostle? Romans 1:1, 1 Corinthians 1:1, 2 Corinthians 1:1, Galatians 1:1, and Ephesians 1:1. Paul owned the title of apostle, but it wasn't just a badge with Paul; it became his new life purpose! His calling to ministry and (as was foretold) his calling to affliction by persecution.

Just know the active life of an apostle is a life of surrender and even suffering. There are many people, in many churches who are called to be apostles, but their denomination won't let them go there, so that key ingredient is left out of the cake. It's simply removed from the Body of believers.

The purpose of this chapter is to remind the Body of Christ that we need God-ordained apostles to edify and lead the Body by example, to train others in the works of the Spirit, and to plant churches if there is a need to. I want to call you apostles out, to help you be open to such a call and find the faith to receive it and walk in it.

Yes, you count the cost and measure it against the blessings of obedience to God. As an apostle, what fruit could you bear for God's kingdom that you aren't bearing now? Seeing people saved? Baptizing? Teaching? Preaching? Discipling? Evangelizing?

Writing to believers and unbelievers?

Apostles are #1 in the five-fold ministry. Ever think about that? Jesus says: *Here, I give you these offices in My Body on Earth.* What are they? Apostles, prophets, evangelists, pastors, and teachers. Look at Ephesians 4:11 (NKJV): "And He Himself [those two words are a chapter in itself, meaning God Himself] gave some *to be* apostles, some prophets, some evangelists, and some pastors and teachers." So God is the one that's determining and giving us apostles and prophets and evangelists and pastors and teachers. God is the One. He, Himself is doing it.

With people today, especially in the African and Apostolic communities, they want to call themselves apostles (I don't mean this in a disrespectful way).

There are way too many self-proclaimed evangelists and self-proclaimed apostles and self-proclaimed prophets. Too many. Then we have pastors that are pastoring a church, but they're evangelistic. There's so much of that. If you really want to level the playing field, you have to look at two things in here (Ephesians 4:11–12, NKJV): (1) "He Himself gave" and (2) these five-fold ministries have a definite purpose they serve. If you look at verse 12, that ends it. What's it for? Says it right there! "For the equipping of the saints for the work of ministry" (NKJV). Period.

Some guy comes up to me and says, "I'm an evangelist."

"Really? What do you mean by that?"

"Well, I mean I'm sharing the Gospel with the lost every week."

"That's not an evangelist."

"But I share the Gospel," he says.

"That's the **ministry of reconciliation** in 2 Corinthians 5:18-19," I reply. We're all called to that, to *be reconciled to God*. If you are an evangelist (according to the Word of God), it is for one reason only: *to equip the saints*. Who are the saints? They're men and women, boys and girls in the Body that are already following Jesus. *The evangelist helps them understand the ministry of reconciliation.* Most folks say Billy Graham was an evangelist. No he wasn't! He was our example of a minister of reconciliation, one of the best!

Evangel-*ism* is the work of reconciling people to God by ministering to those in need of reconciliation. The ministry is to reconcile people to God. *That's* the ministry. *Evangelism* is doing that ministry. The evangelist is called to the church only to equip the saints—to do that ministry (of reconciliation).

It's no different with prophets. It says it in Ephesians 4:12 that prophets are for equipping the saints for the work of ministry, for the edifying of the Body of Christ (the church). These offices, or roles, are not for the lost. Prophets aren't for the lost. They're for the church. So are the apostles, so are pastors, and so are teachers.

Pastors do not shepherd wolves; they shepherd sheep. You can't shepherd wolves. The end of trying to teach and shepherd wolves is to create wolves dressed in sheep's clothing—which is what Jesus warns us to be aware of! You reconcile wolves to God so they can become the sheep of His pasture. Then, and only then, can you shepherd them.

The five-fold ministry are five offices (or roles) that He Himself puts people in. They are for God's Body. Period. That's what they're for. Anything beyond that is man taking way too much leeway with it. Hey, we're all called to be ministers of reconciliation, right? Don't listen to me, let's see what the Word says in 2 Corinthians 5:17–20: "Therefore, if anyone is in Christ, he is a new creation. The old has passed away; behold, the new has come. [Love it!] All this is from God, who through Christ reconciled us to himself and gave us the ministry of reconciliation; that is, in Christ God was reconciling the world to himself, not counting their trespasses against them, and entrusting to us the message of reconciliation. Therefore, we are ambassadors for Christ,

God making his appeal through us. We implore you on behalf of Christ, be reconciled to God." That's our ministry!God making his appeal through us. We implore you on behalf of Christ, be reconciled to God." That's our ministry!

Yeah, but I'm not an outgoing guy like Mike Moore. He could stand up and talk about anything.

OK, assuming that's true, what does it have to do with the ministry of reconciliation? You're sitting at your neighbor's house, and you're to be a minister of reconciliation—to talk to him or her about God. *The end.* We make this *way* too complicated.

Here's an example. When people say of a man, "He's an apostle," pretty soon, other people start referring to him as an apostle. Folks may say, "Come up, Mr. Apostle, and have a word for us." So, if that was you and you don't say anything to the contrary and you get up, the apostle title sticks because a bunch of people have said it. Is God saying it? I don't know, but I see this so much.

Let's differentiate between gifts and the five-fold ministry we were talking about. Where are the gifts mentioned? In 1 Corinthians 12:4–6, it says: "Now there are varieties of gifts, but the same Spirit; and there are varieties of service, but the same Lord; and there are varieties of activities, but it is the same God who empowers them all in everyone." Then in vv. 8–10, it says: "For to one is given through the Spirit the utterance of wisdom, and to another the utterance of knowledge according to the same Spirit, to another faith by the same Spirit, to another gifts of healing by the one Spirit, to another the working of miracles, to another prophecy, to another the ability to distinguish between spirits, to another various kinds of tongues, to another the interpretation of tongues." Those are the gifts.

Now, Romans 12:6–8 says: "Having gifts that differ according to grace given to us, let us use them: if prophecy, in proportion to our faith; if service, in our serving; the one who teaches, in his teaching; the one who exhorts, in exhortation; the one who contributes, with generosity; the one who leads, with zeal; the one who does acts of mercy, with cheerfulness."

So, where's the gift of evangelism? That's not there. The gift of prophecy is: "if prophecy, in proportion to our faith." The gift of teaching is there. I don't see the gift of evangelism in there. It's not. Let's make sure we let Scripture interpret Scripture. OK, it says in Ephesians 4:11 (NKJV): "He gave some *to be* . . . evangelists" (that's a ministry to the church—as opposed to an individual gifting).

Apostles, prophets, evangelists, pastors, and teachers are provided for the Body. Of those five, we can say prophecy is a gift given to individual believers, but just know the office of a prophet is given to the church of Christ. In other words, God can give you or me a word of knowledge to minister to the person in front of us, in the elevator, on the bus. There may be no one else in that person's path when his or her need is the greatest. That's what happened to me while visiting Capetown, South Africa.

I was there with another American named Peter. I know him as a man who has the gift of prophecy. As we were walking near a rock that extends into the ocean, we saw a Black man sitting nearby. I felt something inside, and I said, "Peter, I think I just received a word for that guy. You should go talk to him."

"Why?" he asked. "Because that's your deal."

He replied, "What do you mean *my* deal?"

I explained, "It's what you do and I don't, but I think I just got a word for him."

Peter wisely said, "Well, brother, there's only one way to find out. You go because God gave it to you, not me."

So, I walked up to this Black guy and said, "Hey, brother, we're from the States. It may sound crazy to you, but the Lord has put a real strong message inside me that He wants me to share with you."

The guy looked at me said, "OK, go ahead."

With his permission, I declared, "Something's been stolen from you and it's really big. God wants you to know He's about to return it, but you've got to trust that He can do it."

The man looked at me, and tears started to come out of his eyes. He replied, "I need a moment," and he turned away and wept.

And I knew, at that point, that this was a *God deal*. Beyond the coastline there are hills (overlooking Capetown) that are dotted with amazing (five to twenty-five-million-dollar) homes.

The man pointed up and said, "Look at those hills. Those are the people that stole from me."

I said, "Can I ask you question?"

"Sure."

"How many people do you think are up there with their hands raised to heaven, worshiping Jesus right now?"

"I don't know."

"That's the point—you don't know. There's a lot of rich people that look to Heaven and curse God and a lot of rich people who look to Heaven and praise God. You know what, brother? There's a lot of poor people that do the same—bless God and curse God. It's not about the external; it's about the internal."

We had an amazing conversation, and we ended up praying together!

So you see, God used me for that moment. It was a privilege to minister in a unique way that spoke directly to him; however, I didn't become a prophet that day. I was just a willing vessel to pour out His love to this man in need. That's what God expects all His children to be.

Let's look at Philip, the evangelist. Why do we call him that? Because he led a guy to Christ, right? All he did was expand on the Scriptures to reconcile the Ethiopian eunuch to God through His Son. Let's unpack the whole scene, as recorded for us in Acts 8: 26–39, because he is a model for all of us that are called to be ministers of reconciliation.

"Now an angel of the Lord said to Philip, 'Rise and go toward the south to the road that goes down from Jerusalem to Gaza.' This is a desert place. And he rose and went. And there was an Ethiopian, a eunuch, a court official of Candace, queen of the Ethiopians, who was in charge of all her treasure. He had come to Jerusalem to worship and was returning, seated in his chariot, and he was reading the prophet Isaiah. And the Spirit said to Philip, 'Go over and join this chariot.' So Philip ran to him and heard him reading Isaiah the prophet and asked, 'Do you understand what you are reading?' And he said, 'How can I, unless someone guides me?' And he invited Philip to come up and sit with him. Now the passage of the Scripture that he was reading was this:

'Like a sheep he was led to the slaughter and like a lamb before its shearer is silent, so he opens not his mouth.

In his humiliation justice was denied him. Who can describe his generation?

For his life was taken away from the earth.'

"And the eunuch said to Philip, 'About whom, I ask you, does the prophet say this, about himself or about someone else?' Then Philip opened his mouth, and beginning with this Scripture he told him the good news about Jesus. And as they were going along the road they came to some water, and the eunuch said, 'See, here is water! What prevents me from being baptized?' And Philip said, 'If you believe with all your heart, you may.' And he replied, 'I believe that Jesus Christ is the Son of God.' And he commanded the chariot to stop, and they both went down into the water, Philip and the eunuch, and he baptized him.

And when they came up out of the water, the Spirit of the Lord carried Philip away, and the eunuch saw him no more, and went on his way rejoicing."

First, Philip was **obedient**: God told him to head into the desert, and he went there.

Second, he was **Spirit-led**. The Spirit told him to approach the chariot from Ethiopia, and he did.

Third, he **asked the stranger a question**.

Fourth, he **listened to the stranger** in the chariot.

Fifth, he opened his mouth and **preached Jesus.**

Sixth, he gave the official the **opportunity to confess Jesus** as Lord.

Last, **he baptized** the convert.

Perhaps Philip was called the evangelist because he was encouraging the body of Christ to reconcile the lost to God. He was an evangelist before the eunuch encounter, or they wouldn't have said that. Who said that about Philip? It was Luke in Acts 21:8. He also noted Philip as having four daughters (who prophesied!). Luke said of this man: *he has the office of the evangelist* (no doubt, because Philip was encouraging the Body to go out and reconcile people to God). Let's remember the purpose of the evangelist is to equip the saints.

Jesus gave these five roles, or offices, to the church. It's a package. It's a toolbox with five tools in it. If His Body was a car, He's saying, *I'm giving you an engine that has five cylinders*, and He's telling us, *Use all My cylinders for the benefit of my Body* (the car). There's no giving ourselves a title in there, but we can accept the titles that He gives us to be right with God.

Do you know the title that every believer has? It is "saint." That's why Paul addresses the "saints in Ephesus," the "saints in Colossae," the "saints in Thessalonica." Once we come to Christ, we know, in God's eyes, where are saints. OK? So how's a saint supposed to act? If that's what I am, then how does that make me different than if I wasn't a saint? Being a saint means you are set apart, set apart in Christ.

The Word says in 2 Corinthians 6:17–18: "Therefore go out from their midst, and be separate from them, says the Lord, and touch no unclean thing; then I will welcome you, and I will be a father to you, and you shall be sons and daughters to me, says the Lord Almighty."

The *them* refers to the active sinners in the world. When we do that, get reconciled with God, we become a forgiven sinner. Another name for a forgiven sinner is *saint*. True saints live out their faith and are actively involved in their new ministry of reconciliation!

What we're talking about is being set apart for God's service. Christ set us aside: *Cause you're my kids*.

We're going to send you into that fold (the world) to set more people free.

I DARE YOU to divorce from two things—(1) giving yourself titles to fuel your pride and (2) ignoring when God's calling you to be an apostle, prophet, evangelist, pastor, or teacher—so we can all live out the ministry of reconciliation that is expected of all believers.

We are to go to Christ and be self-replicating, that is, help others go to Christ too! Our lane is to *be available* and ready to share the goodness of God with anybody we meet. In God's eyes, your *availability* is more useful to Him than your *abilities*. The Holy Spirit does all the heavy lifting: *conviction and conversion*. That's the Spirit's lane. Ours is to be ready, willing, and able (equipped) to share both the Word and our testimony with a dying world.

Don't sit in the boat when God's called you to walk on the water.
– Popular sermon meme

For if while we were enemies we were reconciled to God by the death of his Son, much more, now that we are reconciled, shall we be saved by his life.
– Romans 5:10

May you live out the titles that God gives all believers: saints, living messengers, ambassadors of Christ, His children, the sheep of His pasture, the Bride of Christ, and so much more!

Part IV

THE FINAL MASTERPIECE

22

REAL LOVE IS IN FORGIVING

LUKE 7:36 introduces us to a Pharisee named Simon, a religious leader, like the rabbi of the town, the guy that read the Torah every day, that knew all the rules and regulations. He had it all down pat. He knew what you were supposed to do and not supposed to do. One day, he invites Jesus who's this prophet, this important person. He was probably thinking: *I'll invite this new rabbi to my house. I've got a lot of money and influence. Certainly He'll show up.*

So Jesus goes there, and there's this woman that (the Word says) lived a sinful life. What does that mean? Does it mean she's a prostitute who sold her body? Does that mean she was known for sexual favors? We don't know what "sinful life" means. We all have sin in our life. We all do! How do I know that? Because we're not perfect. We often do something that we think is right, but it's not. We do a lot of stuff out of ignorance, and we do a lot of stuff willfully.

In an effort to protect ourselves, we learn protective behaviors in life. The protection mechanism causes us to do things (we think) out of innocence, but if we didn't have that protective measure in the first place, we probably wouldn't have done it.

It's like the story about a hole in the street. There's a hole in the street, and everybody knows if you fall in the hole you'll never be seen again. So, what do people end up doing? They build a fence around the hole, and they won't drive down the street where the hole is. They won't let their kids near the hole, and (at the end of the day) the hole ends up controlling their life.

Now everything revolves around the hole: *Got to stay away from the hole.* Then years go by, and you're in college and they teach you: *Remember the hole. You can't go there! There's a hole in the street.*

Everybody's focused on what you're *not* supposed to do (get near the hole). That, then, drives your life—staying away from the hole.

It's no different with us. We have our patterns in life that we use as we walk out life. Most of the time, we're fearful of certain things, and we've learned not to do certain things.

It's like the *fence laws* that the Jews used. They know the Torah says, "Don't commit adultery." They say: *Well, that's easy; we'll make a fence law.* What's a fence law? *A man can't be within fifteen feet of a woman.* Talk about social distancing! That was done centuries before the coronavirus pandemic.

They reasoned that if you don't walk within fifteen feet of a woman, you can't commit adultery. *There, (they felt) we got that one covered.* Except the Lord Jesus spoke in Matthew 5, and He said: *Guys, you've heard that it was said, you've heard that it was said, you've heard that it was said* . . . six times He begins that way during the Sermon on the Mount. What He's saying is: *I'm raising the bar so high that you can't construct a fence around the outside because you need to deal with what's inside of you.*

Jesus isn't telling the crowd that it's wrong to make an effort; He's saying you *can't* do it. You can't keep the Seventh Commandment to not commit adultery. He says: *I'm looking at the heart and that can't be tamed . . . it can't.* When a person confesses Jesus as Savior and Lord, God gives that person a new heart. He or she goes from a heart of stone to a heart of flesh that God gives. This spiritual heart surgery is explained in the Book of Ezekiel 36:26. Not only does God take the stony heart out, but He also *puts a new spirit in us, as well as the heart of flesh.*

With that backdrop of a sinful life (whatever that means), the woman that came to the Pharisee's house walked in, and Simon thought: *Oh man, He doesn't know who this woman is! If this guy was a Prophet, He'd know who's touching Him and what kind of woman she is. She is a sinner.* Simon didn't call her a prostitute or a whore; he called her a sinner. (Like he wasn't?)

There are two things in this parable we have to look at: *judgment* and *comparison*. Those are the two things that come up. We need to divorce ourselves from comparison. We need to divorce ourselves from judgment because what did this man do? In his mind, he said: *I know your behavior. I'm judging your behavior. I know what you do. I'm making a judgment.*

First, he also looked at Jesus, and he made a judgment of Jesus by thinking: *If you were really a prophet (like everybody says you are), You would know who this woman is, but you don't. So I'm judging your ability to know right from wrong. I'm judging your ability to discern the character of who's around you, and if You can't discern this, maybe your disciples are the same way.* The guy's making all these judgments (internally), but this thinking and judging fit the profile of Simon because for a guy to say what he said, you know there's a lot more going on inside him.

Second, he's comparing his life as a Pharisee and keeping the Law perfectly (in his mind) to this woman who does things that he would never do. However, he's probably thought them *in his heart* (enough times) that he already did them!

At least this woman wasn't trying to hide. This Pharisee was really good at hiding, at keeping the outside of the cup looking clean. What's interesting is, after this very brief encounter, the woman walks in and does all these humble things, so Jesus says: "Simon, I have something to tell you."

"Tell me teacher," Simon replies (now he calls Him teacher).

Jesus continues His lesson on judgment: *Two people owed money to a master; one owed five thousand dollars, and the other owed five hundred dollars.*

Neither had the money, so the master said, "I forgive you both." Which of them would love the master more?

Simon, the smart Pharisee said, *I suppose the one who had the bigger debt forgiven.*

Jesus says, *Yes, you've judged rightly.*

I love the way He said: "You have judged rightly" (Luke 7:43). It pointed out an obvious contrast. Simon was judging before, and now the Lord could say: *You judged right this time*, which implies he didn't judge right the first time. Jesus threw a softball fact pattern so Simon could make a sound judgment and knock it out of the park.

Finally, Jesus completes his host's Judgment 101 class by saying: *Hey Simon, see this woman? I'm in your home, but you didn't give me water for my feet.* That was the number one thing, back in those days, when you entered someone's home.

There were two things that could happen if you came as a guest at a Hebrew home. Number one, if the hosts had money, a servant would be sitting at the door to wash your feet for you. Why? Because everybody wore open sandals, and it was dusty. Their feet got dirty quickly. They didn't have paved roads like we do today. So they would wash the guest's feet and clean them in a bucket of water. Or, two, if the host didn't have servants, water would be in a basin and guests could wash their own feet.

When Jesus walked into the Pharisee's house, no water was provided, so Jesus said: *You didn't give Me any water, but this woman? She took her tears, and that was the water she cleaned My feet with. Then she wiped them, not with a towel but with her hair. She took the dirt from My feet and put it on her hair. She used water that came from her body out of being so broken about her life. You didn't kiss Me.* (In that culture, men would greet each other with a kiss on the cheek.) Simon neglected that, so Jesus testifies: *From the time I entered, she kissed My feet. You didn't put oil on Me* (a custom for special guests), *but she poured perfume on my feet. Therefore, I tell you, her many sins have been forgiven—as her great love has shown. But whoever has been forgiven little loves little.* Jesus looked her in the eyes and said: "Your sins are forgiven" (Luke 7:48).

Simon is thinking: *Who is this that forgives sins?*

Jesus told her: "Go in peace" (Luke 7:50). She came in turmoil, broken, hoping for an answer, and because she encountered Jesus, she left in peace. Not her peace, but His peace, His shalom.

Can we just take a timeout for a second? Do you have peace with God, or are you in turmoil? If the answer is turmoil, how's that workin' for ya? I've been there. I know how it worked for me and my closest friends: divorce, thoughts of suicide, addictions. That's not peace by any standard. When is enough, enough?

Three paths emanate from the turmoil in our life: denial, depression, or godly sorrow. Simon is Mr. Denial. He thinks he's gold as far is God's concerned. He's too into himself to even realize he's on death row. Denial requires myopic vision (not really seeing the whole picture) and an unwillingness to be teachable—and to change as a result of what God has shown you.

Depression is not on display in this account, but it is one of the three responses we can't ignore. My guess is there is a cultural influence that didn't allow depression to plague the Jews like it does in our modern society.

All depression has within it a sense of hopelessness. The more our culture moves away from Jesus, the onset of depression grows exponentially! What do many Christians sing? "My hope is built on nothing less / Than Jesus' blood and righteousness / I dare not trust the sweetest frame / But wholly lean on Jesus' name." So you see, when Jesus is ripped out of our societal fabric, our rock of hope goes with Him. And that leaves only depression or denial to cope with the hard things in life.

The so-called sinner woman realized she was on death row every day. It was a massive burden to her. She let it have the best effect on her possible—and that was to be broken via godly sorrow. Godly sorrow ALWAYS leads to brokenness. If you walk away with only regret for your actions, then you can be sure you're not on the godly sorrow bus. Mere regret is satan's last distraction to keep you from brokenness and the benefits of godly sorrow. The question is: Will you go there with her, or will you be like Simon, deny the problem (or solution), and try to *fake it till you make it?* Jesus is clear with Simon and with us: *There is no making it that way. It still leads to death.*

What I love is that this woman knew herself. *I am not that good, Jesus. You are good.* And she went for it. She knew there was something here to change her life forever.

Conversely, Simon is telling himself: *I'm good. I keep the Law. I'm not like that deplorable woman.* Jesus, in love, says: *You think you're good, Simon. You don't know how bad you are. Therefore, you won't love that much because you don't know how much you've been forgiven.*

As we go back to this scene in Simon's house, we see comparison, we see judgment, and there's a huge takeaway (for us) about love expressed by forgiveness. When we realize we're all felons before God (deserving the death penalty for the felonies we have committed against God), that should rock our boat. We have to get to a point in our lives where we stop looking at the sins (that *emanate* from our nature) and really drill down on our nature. What will we find? That our nature is hellbent against God.

That's our nature. *Our* nature.

The problem with human morality today is that morality doesn't need God. Humanistic morality says: *I live a moral life. I can determine good from evil.*

The problem is we're sitting at the (proverbial) tree of the knowledge of good and evil, thinking we can reason our way through what we're doing and can actually reason our way into knowing right from wrong.

The Lord says: *You can't determine right from wrong.*

You don't have that ability. I have to show you. That's why, when Adam and Eve ate from that tree of the knowledge of good and evil, the Lord said: *Did you eat from that tree that I told you not eat from? Now you think you can reason your way between right and wrong, but you can't. You were lied to.*

Now, we're ready for the essence of this chapter (and I think it's huge)—namely, dealing with *the love*.

We're talking about the love the woman had for Jesus, the love He had for her, and the love He had for Simon. Both of His expressions of love were tied to forgiveness. *Don't miss that.* Because if we can realize how much we have been forgiven (what that looks like), we can't help but lovingly cling to Jesus—Who did all the heavy lifting so we could be at peace with God, at peace with ourselves, and at peace with our neighbors.

Your eternal life is too important to play Simon Says.

Simon says: I'm a good person.

Simon says: He or she is not a good person.

Simon says: God owes me!

Instead, I recommend you play Sinner Says: *Sinner says*: I am not a good person. There is no good in me.

Sinner says: I am too low to judge anybody.

Sinner says: I owe God!

See the difference? Now let's take a field trip with Jesus to the Temple in His day. In Luke 18, He describes two men entering the Temple. One guy is popular and highly esteemed in Hebrew society. The other is called a "publican." That means he's a tax collector, like our buddy Zach who climbed the tree. The term *publican* is also used with the pejorative term *heathen*. Here's Jesus's parable:

"Two men, a Pharisee and a publican, went up into the temple to pray.

The Pharisee stood and prayed like this: 'God, I thank You that I am not as other men are: extortioners, unjust, adulterers, or even as this publican. I fast twice a week, and I give tithes of all that I possess.'

And the publican, standing far off, dared not gaze up to heaven but beat upon his chest, saying: 'God be merciful to me, a sinner.'

I tell you, the publican, rather than the other man, went down to his house justified. For every one that exalts himself shall be humbled; and those that humble themselves shall be exalted." Luke 18:10-14

When we look at Simon, we see judgment, we see the pitfalls of comparison. The bigger lesson for us here (that people often overlook) is this whole area of love. This woman loved. But why? What does that mean, that *she loved*? It is a love based on: *I am so forgiven, I am free! The Savior of mankind, the creator of human flesh—who created life—loves me!* He loves me so much that He says: "I'm not holding anything against you."

In 2 Corinthians 5:19, it says, "God was in Christ reconciling the world unto Himself" (KJV). Then He goes on to make a very outrageous statement: *not counting their sin against them*. If the creator of the universe (Christ) says: *I don't count your sin against you*, then how can we count sin against other people that have offended us? How could we say, *I'm holding this against you*, when God says, *I'm **not** holding that against them*? Why are you holding that against them? More importantly, *why do you hold sin against yourself*? What's your *why* behind the *what*? Ponder this question as you look into the eyes of Jesus and hear Him say: *Why have you looked at yourself and not forgiven yourself when I've already forgiven you at the cross?*

Self-forgiveness is probably one of the biggest areas that the enemy wants to keep us from because, once we have been forgiven and we know the depth of the forgiveness from the sin nature that we have, we will learn how to love ourselves in the way God designed us to love.

When we can receive His unconditional mercy, grace, and love for us, we will learn righteous self-love.

Then, clearly, we will be able to love other people. It starts with us learning to love ourselves.

That's very difficult for many people. *How do I love myself? How can I love you if I don't love me?* I can't. It's impossible! *And how can I love me, unless I know that the manufacturer of the human race has forgiven me?*

From the description of the woman at Simon's house, her prior existence seems like the country song that goes: "Looking for love in all the wrong places." That aimless search was the likely source of her sin.

Her *love train* was on the wrong tracks. As Jesus gave Simon the opportunity to make a sound judgment after he messed up, He also gave the woman the opportunity to love rightly and righteously after she messed up. The "old" Simon judged wrongly. The "old" woman loved wrongly. Jesus gave them the wind in their sails to course-correct when they needed it so badly. He does that for us too!

Just know the greatest ships on the oceans cannot be steered unless they are moving, so move towards God. Move away from self-judgment to self-forgiveness. Move away from selfish pride to selfless love.

A big key is how love and forgiveness are tied together because John 3:16 says: "For God so loved the world that he gave his only begotten Son" (KJV). He sent His Son to die on a cross for forgiveness of sin, so love and forgiveness are tied together. I love the word *so* in John 3:16. The proof of *so* is what follows—the word *that*. God *so* loved the world *that* He gave His only Son. (What more was there to give?)

This woman *so* loved Jesus *that* she washed His feet with her tears, wiped them clean with her hair, kissed His feet repeatedly, and anointed them with oil. She *so* loved Him, and we know why. The word *so* takes love to a whole different level. There's tenderness in that word.

God the Son realized: *My love is so intense that I want to forgive them. I want to die for their sin.* It's so intense, and it's tied together with God.

God wants to forgive us! People think: *He's so strict and He has His rules and He's going to judge us all.* No. Stop! Go to the opposite side of that—all those animal sacrifices in Leviticus God had in place because He wants to forgive people

By the many Old Testament offerings, He's telling us: *I want to, I need to forgive you because I love you so much! It's part of who I Am.* He's eager to say: *I forgive you, son. I forgive you My precious daughter.* Besides holier-than-thou Simon, who doesn't want and need that?

There are many people that raise their fist at God and say: *I don't need your forgiveness. I'm perfectly fine. I'm a good person, I do yoga twice a week, whatever.* God is saying: *I love you. You need My forgiveness, and the enemy's blinded you in such a way that you don't see how much you need My forgiveness!* Still, many people say, by their actions: *I don't need your forgiveness.*

How well do you know God? Are you tracking with Him? Do you care to track with Him by reading His Word?

I DARE YOU to divorce from comparing yourself with others and judging others. It is spiritual folly that never has a good outcome or a happy ending.

> The only person you should try to be better than is the person you were yesterday.
> **– Matty Mullins**

> "Then [the King] shall say to those on his left, 'Depart from me, you cursed, into eternal fire prepared for the devil and his angels. For I was an hungry and you gave me no food, I was thirsty and you gave me no drink, I was a stranger, and you did not welcome me, naked and you did not clothe me, sick and in prison and you did not visit me.' Then they will also answer, saying, 'Lord, when did we see you hungry or thirsty or a stranger or naked or sick or in prison, and did not minister to you?' Then he will answer them, saying, 'Truly,

I say to you, as you did not do it to one of the least of these, you did not do it to me."
– Matthew 25:41–45

May you so love Jesus that you give your heart and life to Him in total faith, trust, and surrender.

23

ALONG COMES MARY

GOD'S WORD IS FULL OF WOMEN who have beauty, bravery, boldness, and outstanding character. I want to introduce you to three of them named Mary. *Why these three?* Because they each experienced Jesus in a way that we can learn so much from. They each related to Jesus uniquely. To one Mary, Jesus was her son. To another Mary, Jesus was her hero and rescuer. To the third Mary, Jesus was her friend.

(Side note: I don't know of another religion that honors, cherishes, and dignifies women as God's Word and the true Body of Christ does.)

Let's start with Mary, the mother of Jesus. She was the earthly mother of God's only begotten Son. She bore Jesus out of her blessed womb. Of them all, this Mary had the most unique relationship with Jesus. To begin to appreciate this, we should look at who she was before she met (and named) Jesus. She was a virgin. She never had relations with a man, yet she was engaged to a carpenter named Joseph. In that culture, engagement/betrothal meant you're committed to marriage and you're going to be faithful until the day of the wedding ceremony.

She listens as the angel Gabriel comes to her and says: *Be of good cheer! You are highly favored. The Lord is with you. Blessed are you among women and blessed will be the fruit of your womb.* Mary was so overwhelmed by this strange greeting and didn't know what to make of it. Gabriel interrupts her thoughts with an admonition and affirmation: "Do not be afraid, Mary, for you have found favor with God" (Luke 1:30). What an unspeakable blessing her ears heard a second time: *You are favored by the Almighty!* Immediately, her fear goes away, and she adopts this call of God on her life and says to the angel: *Behold, I am the handmaid of the Lord. Be it to me as you have said.* One takeaway from this is Mary is embracing the angel's prophecy and committing to live out God's will.

Just know that this favor of God came at a huge personal cost to Mary. At the end of so many months, she was obviously pregnant and (just as obviously) not married. Everyone in her city concluded she had broken her betrothal vow to Joseph and was guilty of fornication, or worse . . . adultery. She went from *hero to zero* in their eyes. Under Jewish law, she could be stoned for what they were sure she had done. The first stone would have been cast by fiancé Joseph, but he didn't go there because the angel of the Lord told him (in a dream) that she conceived of the Holy Ghost and that she had sex with no man. Rather than imposing a death sentence on her, he announced he would marry her. In essence, Joseph saved Mary's life (because of the angel).

As you probably know, Jesus was falsely accused when He was taken to the Roman governor Pontius Pilate for judgment. Why do I bring that up? Because we fail to remember that this falsely accused man was the son of a falsely accused mother! All her life, people considered her firstborn son an illegitimate child. What did that say about her? It was the T-shirt she wore (and the humility that goes with it) till the day she died. Next takeaway: be willing to be misunderstood for knowing Jesus.

Another takeaway is Mary's utter confidence in Jesus and His power as the Son of God. Before Jesus had done any miracles, He, His Mom, and His disciples attended a wedding in Cana (Galilee). Towards the end of the festivities, the wine had run out. That is not supposed to happen and was a major cultural faux pas in that day. No doubt, Mary felt sorry for the host family. With confidence, she spoke to her Son and said: "They have no wine" (John 2:3). Seemingly taken aback, Jesus replied: *What's that got to do with Me? My time has not come yet* (to reveal His powers of divinity). Like a good Jewish mother, Mary did not take His version of no for an answer. Instead, she looked at the servants standing nearby and said: "Do whatever he tells you" (John 2:5). With that, Jesus told them to fill six stone waterpots with water. When they did, He said: *Draw a ladle out and give it to the overseer of the feast* (like a wedding coordinator).

They did, and the overseer was so amazed at the quality of wine he tasted that he called the groom over to school him: *You always serve the best wine first. Then, when the guests get a little tipsy you bring out the lesser wine; but you have saved this exquisite wine for last!* At that moment, the disciples of Jesus knew they weren't just following a unique rabbi; they also were following God in the flesh! Mary must have had a smile on her face and a great sense of satisfaction to see her Son in action. Our last takeaway from this Mary is to confidently ask Jesus for a miracle when one is needed.

Thirty years after Mary gave birth to Jesus, Mary Magdalene entered the scene. In Luke, chapter 8, we read that Jesus had cast seven demons out of her.

Mary Magdalene came to Jesus with a sense of humility: *Lord, You don't know who I am. I'm a bad* woman. I think bad thoughts and do nasty things. *In essence, Jesus said: No, that's not what I see in you, Mary, because you have humbled yourself. You're asking me to deliver you and forgive you. You're delivered. Your demons have gone out to never return. You're forgiven, Mary. You will walk with Me.* And Mary embraced His assurances. She got a new identity in Christ. From then on, she and other women assisted in Christ's ministry as they could.

Of all the Jewish young women in history, the angel Gabriel came to Mary, the fiancé of Joseph. Of all the Jewish people living after the Crucifixion, Mary Magdalene was the first human Jesus appeared to after He rose again! Not to one of His apostles, but to Mary. One of the reasons she got that honor was her proximity. She went to Jesus's grave the Sunday after His burial Thursday at dusk. She had been at His cross four days before, and now she was at His tomb. In life and in death, Mary was all in for Jesus. What is the takeaway from Mary Magdalene? She is the picture of whole-hearted devotion to the Lord, her Savior.

The final Mary was a dear friend of Jesus. He visited her home when He came to Bethany to visit Lazarus, along with Martha (Mary's older sister). On one visit, we observe the scene that depicts Mary's heart.

Martha was making sure preparations were right throughout the house. She wanted everything right:

Mary, the Messiah is coming here. This is Jesus.

Don't you get this? Martha's preparing the food and wants to make sure everything is ideal for everybody. (Nothing wrong with that.) But when Mary stopped being Martha's kitchen go-fer to listen to Jesus talk, Martha interrupted the Lord to try to enlist Jesus into telling Mary to get back to work: *Jesus, can you tell Mary to do something? I'm trying to make this right for everybody.* Jesus, in his love, said: *Martha, you're just worried and bothered. Though you have good intentions, you're focusing on the wrong thing. All of this will take care of itself.*

He wasn't saying don't continue with the preparations. He was saying: *Your attitude behind the preparations is not right, Martha.* Having read this book, we know Martha's *why* behind the *what* was off. **Jesus sees our why**. Her why wasn't right. Mary had a different why: *I am with the Messiah. He's speaking. I've got to learn. I need to know Him better.* Jesus said of Mary: *She desired the better thing.*

Martha desired to be known as an excellent hostess. It was about her. Mary desired to know more of Jesus. It was about Him. Our takeaway from this Mary is: never believe you've got Jesus all figured out. Always seek to know more of Him.

Days, weeks, or months later, Mary's brother Lazarus fell gravely ill. His sisters immediately sent for Jesus, but

He was a three-day journey away. The urgent message was given to the Lord, and right away . . .Jesus . . . stays put! It was not His time to go back there, but two days later it was. By the time Jesus arrived at the outskirts of the town of Bethany, Lazarus has been dead and buried for four days! The scene at Mary's house was one of weeping, grief, and anguish. Because Bethany is less than two miles from Jerusalem, many came from there to console the sisters over their loss.

Word reached Mary that Jesus was waiting for her outside of town. She quickly reached Him and fell at His feet, saying: *Lord, if You were here earlier, my brother would not have died.* He inquired where the grave was and was led there. This is where you find the shortest verse in scripture: "Jesus wept" (John 11:35). It turns out the grave was actually a cave with a stone sealing the entrance. Jesus said: *Remove the stone.* Martha questioned why Jesus said that, but Mary did not. She was trusting God for a miracle.

When the stone was rolled away, Jesus commanded (in a loud voice): *Lazarus come out of there*, and Mary's brother (still in his graveclothes) walked out of the tomb! That scene was one of shock and awe. What I purposefully omitted telling you is that Martha was the first sister to meet Jesus outside of Bethany.

She, too, said that if only He had been there, her brother would still be alive, but she added this: *But I* know that, even now, whatever You ask of God,– He shall give it to You. Her words said: *From my understanding of You, I think You can raise my brother up.* Mary never made such an affirmation to Jesus, yet when it was time for the rubber to meet the road (taking away the stone), it was Martha who doubted and Mary who believed. In other words, Martha *talked the talk* but Mary *walked the walk*. God wants us to walk the walk— to move from head knowledge and move into actual experiences with God (in faith). Knowing about God results from *observation*; being used of God results from *participation*. What are you—a doer or a watcher (from a safe distance)?

These three Marys, so different in outward expression, were exactly the same internally. They all had a humble attitude, and experienced mercy and grace. They got to receive that from the Father by His Son. They were Mary, the mother of Jesus; Mary the faithful follower of Jesus; and Mary the friend of Jesus.

I DARE YOU to divorce from any attitude of looking down on women because of their gender and to apply (in your life) what these three amazing women have taught us:

To embrace prophecy and commit to doing God's will;

To be willing to be misunderstood for Him and have confidence in His power (to save and heal);
To ask Jesus for a miracle;
To have whole-hearted devotion to Jesus;
To seek to know more of Jesus; and
To walk the walk instead of talk the talk.

> For God to mend your broken heart you must give Him all the pieces.
> **– Rick Warren**

> *For if, because of one man's trespass, death reigned through that one man, much more will those who receive the abundance of grace and the free gift of righteousness reign in life through one man Jesus Christ.*
> **– Romans 5:17**

May you pattern your relationship with Christ after the humility, confidence, expectation, and devotion of these three Marys.

24

FOURTEENTH GENERATION

IT'S INTERESTING HOW DIVERSE the Scriptures are. Some parts are so different that we may ask ourselves: *Why is this here?* We probably don't even read it, or if we do, we just scan through it. This often happens when you find a genealogy: Abraham begot Isaac, Isaac begot Jacob, and so on. Most people reading a genealogy in God's Word move on to get past that because they want to get into something else. But the genealogies are there for a reason.

Matthew's Gospel (first chapter) goes through the genealogy of Christ, beginning with Abraham. At the end it says: "So all the generations from Abraham to David were fourteen generations, and from David to the deportation to Babylon fourteen generations, and from the deportation to Babylon to the Christ fourteen generations" (Matthew 1:17). Forty-two total, right? I don't know about you, but numbers fascinate me. So, to be clear, I counted up from Abraham to David: fourteen; David to the Babylonian captivity: fourteen; Babylonian captivity to Jesus: thirteen. *What?* I did it again and counted fourteen, fourteen, and thirteen! As a result, I asked the Lord a question: "Where is the fourteenth generation?" It's got to be fourteen. The Word can't be wrong!

God spoke to my spirit: *You are the fourteenth generation,* and He explained to me: *In Jesus, the church is the fourteenth generation. You're the last generation in those Scriptures.* I'm thinking: *Oh my goodness, we are the fourteenth generation.* We are the generation that God spoke about two thousand years ago. It was as if Jesus was telling me: *You are the fourteenth. I lived with Joseph, the thirteenth, but in Me is fourteen. I gave my birthright to My church.* The Holy Spirit went out and found a bride for Jesus: *it's you and me.* It's people that will *confess with their mouth Jesus is Lord and believe in their heart that God raised (them) from the dead.* We are the fourteenth generation! That's almost too much to wrap our minds around!

What does that mean to be the fourteenth generation? Our names are inscribed on His hands. God had the first tattoo . . . and it's our name. (See Isaiah 49:16.) We are that generation. We get to carry out the Kingdom of God on planet Earth. Our struggle is not against flesh and blood. God is not fighting satan. He is not in a battle with satan or the demonic or the rulers and principalities and powers (which are all plural in the book of Ephesians). They're rulers; they're demonic.

We struggle against them, not God. He made them. They are created beings, but God is eternal. He's giving us His word: *You fight that battle!* That's why we have the full armor of God: the helmet of salvation, the breastplate of righteousness, footwear of the preparation of the Gospel, as well as the sword of the Spirit. It's all in front of us (nothing on your backside) because we move forward as the fourteenth generation. *Right now!*

This is especially in the States, where the manifestation of evil is greater now than we've ever seen in our lifetimes! Evil has been around, but the manifestation of what we're seeing is evidenced by the fact that law and order is breaking down in the United States: drug use is up, murders and violent crime are up, illegal alien infiltration is up, suicides are up, cities and counties are defunding their peace officers, so-called sanctuary cities are releasing jailed illegals without notifying US immigration authorities. How can law and order *not* be breaking down? As a result, believers (the fourteenth generation) should be crying out (right now) against what's happening. We're in trouble.

We are the fourteenth generation. We are a people of destiny! Yet there are followers of Jesus that don't understand this. That's because they don't read the Word of God. They just know Jesus died on a cross. *That's a great start!*

My first point is that it isn't enough to believe (mentally assent) that God exists. Folks, the book of James tells us that even the demons believe in God! Believing in God (alone) does not make a person saved, or the demons would be saved, right? Our beliefs mean nothing if they don't guide how we live our lives and treat other people. Beliefs guide our actions. Thoughts and feelings are fluid. By nature, they should not influence our actions if they go against our core beliefs.

My second point is that we mustn't let our biased terms for God ruin our ability to care for others who don't tend to use our preferred terms. Case in point: I spoke to an Uber driver (who was a Muslim) and said: "May I pray for you?"

He answered: "Well, sure."

I said: "I want to pray for you in the name of a prophet. His name is Isa [EE-sah]. He's in the Koran, you know that, right?"

He admitted: "I don't read the Koran a lot, but I know about the prophet Mohammed."

"What about the prophet Isa? Have you heard of Him?"

"Yes, I have."

I explained: "That's Jesus."

"Yes, I know."

I said: "I want to pray to Allah right now. May I do that for you? And I'm going to pray in the name of the Prophet Isa that God is going to appear to you in white in a dream, and that's Isa, that's Jesus."

Did you know that many Muslim men and women are experiencing Jesus in dreams? In all reported cases, He is dressed in white. That's why I prayed that way. I would ask that you not be offended that I called God Allah in this man's presence. It's no different from Arabs calling Jesus Isa. Same Person, different language. That's all.

Let's be honest . . . Mary did not name her miracle son Jesus. She was not a Roman. She was a Hebrew who gave Him the Hebrew name the angel Gabriel told her to give: Yeshua. It's a derivative of the Hebrew name Joshua. In America, we have adopted the Roman name, Jesus. So, let's not get uppity about a name like Allah because that would make us verifiable hypocrites.

What I've learned is we must take the terms, the way we communicate (as the fourteenth generation) and be as wise as serpents but as innocent as doves. We have to speak people's languages as best we can. The apostle Paul did that when he went into Greece. He connected with the thinkers and philosophers of that day.

Whenever you speak to a Muslim, speak about Jesus ("Isa"). They want to hear about Jesus, not Christianity. Jesus was not a Christian. Man, let's get rid of that concept. He's the Son of the Most-High God that came to planet Earth to take away the sin of the world. That's why Jesus came. He didn't come to judge the world; He came to save the world by His blood.

We want to jump behind a belief system and name it Christianity, which (historically) is diametrically opposed to Muslims. People think of extreme Christians and think of extreme Muslims as they remember the Crusades. No wonder Muslims have a coping mechanism that keeps them away from Christians. To them, we wear the black hats (to use a Texas analogy).

The vast majority of Muslim people are not trying to throw bombs at us or blow themselves up. They're content in following their Muslim faith in Allah—what little they may know of him and the Koran.

We've got to learn to talk to people—where we are not afraid of what we're saying to them, or how they will react to the name of Jesus.

Hey, I've been on the wrong side of categorizing people, and it rendered me so ineffective for the Kingdom. One day, I was relaxing at a pool (during a company event) and met a young couple doing the same. I was talking to the woman, and I assumed she was married to this guy. Later, she announced to me, "We're both gay." I was taken aback by my misread. She sensed that and said, "Tell me what you're feeling right now." I could only say, "You know what? I don't know."

That turned out to be a really good question for me to grapple with because I wanted to hide behind Christianity. I wanted to hide behind the terminology and got a false sense of: *Well, Lord, it's You and me against these people.* It is ironic (at best) or idiotic (at worst) for us to try to enlist God to be against the people we don't care for when He is, and always will be, the God of love for all people of His creation! We've got to break these barriers of communication (this terminology comfort-food we eat) and stop looking at a non-believing world (that has no clue of salvation) and condemning them for their behavior. *What else are they supposed to do?* They're not even saved yet! We're trying to change their behavior.

THAT'S NOT THE GOAL. The goal is for us to learn to love them and love them and love them as Jesus would and approach people as He would.

Why? Because we are the fourteenth generation. There should be something inside our hearts that asks: *What does that mean, Lord? What do you want me to do? What does that mean today (in the twenty-first century) for me if I'm that fourteenth generation?*

When I get the realization that I've been chosen to live in *this time* with what's going on, then I can begin to appreciate the enormity of the responsibility I have to this dying world.

As I write this chapter, in the ninth month of the year, over forty-one million people have died in 2021! How many were saved? How many were ushered into a miserable eternity because they did not know Isa, they did not know Yeshua? In other words, they did not know Jesus.

Of course we ask the question WHY? Why did they not know Jesus? The apostle Paul, in Romans 10:13, says: "For 'everyone who calls on the name of the Lord will be saved.'" That's cool. What a blessing! However, he continues down a logic trail: "How then will they call on him in whom they have not believed? And how are they to believe in him of whom they have never heard? And how are they to hear without someone preaching? And how are they to preach, unless they are sent? As it is written, 'How beautiful are the feet of those who preach the good news!' But they have not all obeyed the gospel. For [the prophet] Isaiah says, 'Lord, who has believed what he has heard from us?' So faith comes from hearing, and hearing through the word of Christ" (Romans 10:14–17).

At times, I wish I was around when Jesus began His three years of ministering on Earth. What a blessed generation that was. Or what about that final generation of Hebrews that were slaves to the Egyptians? They experienced the promised Passover and were not only released to their freedom but also lavished with lots of Egyptian gold, silver, and precious things as they left! It was the greatest transfer of wealth from one people group to another that the world has ever seen. The Hebrews got to cross the Red Sea on dry ground! What a blessed generation that was!

However, those generations do not compare to being in the generation when Jesus returns in His glory. Is that not during the fourteenth generation? Since Jesus ascended to Heaven, the world has waited two millennia for such a time as this.

WE are the chosen ones. We are His priesthood! We can't keep God to ourselves. If we are bold or society moves against Christ, we get to fellowship in His sufferings so we can fully bask in the glory of His presence and place crowns at His feet in Heaven!

There is no better time to be alive than *now*. There is no greater responsibility for reaching the lost than *now*. Not just the lost in India and China (with a combined population of 2.8 billion, compared to 334 million in the United States) but also the lost person next door, at work, at school, at the park, in the grocery store, or at the soccer game.

Let's man up (as believers) to the unique calling of the fourteenth generation! It is our honor, it is our calling, and it is our destiny! With the power of Christ, this generation will not fail to do what it has been called to do, namely, to stand firm in the Lord under all circumstances, use our giftings, and live out the ministry of reconciliation we looked at in Chapter 21, "Apostle 13."

I DARE YOU to divorce from having a cavalier attitude about the Day of Judgment and the second Coming of Christ. Instead, put on the full armor of God to accomplish what only the fourteenth generation has been tasked to accomplish. The world is not ready for His return. We get ourselves ready, and we help as many as we can get ready too!

> "The gospel is only good news if it gets there in time."
> **– Carl F. H. Henry**

> *For [God] says, "In a favorable time I listened to you, and in a day of salvation I helped you." Behold, now is the favorable time; behold, now is the time of salvation.*
> **– 2 Corinthians 6:2**

May you be bold and ready to share the good news with those around you in season and out of season.

There is no fifteenth generation. It's up to you. It's up to us!

25

DON'T HAVE A PRAYER?

THERE IS A DARE at the end of each chapter. You know what rhymes with dare? *Prayer.* That's what this chapter is about because you will fail every dare in this book if you don't go into it, go through it, and go beyond it with prayer, trusting God all the way.

Otherwise, *you don't have a prayer* at completing the dare. That's not just a rhyme but also a reality.

How many ways are there to pray? Some recite a prayer by rote, some read it from a book or the Internet, some have a consistent pattern, some pray Scriptures (like the Lord's Prayer), some pray in an unknown language, and some just pray "as they are led," where each one is different. I'm not talking about all that.

There are only two ways to pray:

1. Believing in faith
2. Hoping yet doubting

In business, we have a saying that is true about investment securities, real estate, car purchases, timeshares, travel deals, whatever! That saying is: *No deal is better than a bad deal*. It helps us walk away from toxic sales or purchases that will eat away at us via seller or buyer remorse.

I'm here to tell you: *No prayer is better than a faithless prayer*. Why waste God's time, and yours, with a prayer that has zero faith behind it? There's a name for that: *a wish*. That reminds me of another saying: *If wishes were horses, beggars would ride*. That adage is to encourage us to work for what we dream about. The Word explains how we are to pray: "And without faith it is impossible to please him, for whoever would draw near to God must believe that he exists and that he rewards those who seek him" (Hebrews 11:6).

Let's break down these principles (not laws):

1. A lack of faith displeases God (because we know abundant faith pleases Him).
2. We need to believe God exists and He hears our prayers.
3. God rewards those who really go after Him.

You can read books about prayer that will discuss various *positions* of prayer—standing, kneeling, prostrate, and so on—but I see only one position of prayer, and that is *the position of faith*. If we don't pray in faith, it doesn't matter if you're on your knees, standing, on your face, or sitting in a vehicle. James 1:5–7 makes it crystal clear: "If any of you lacks wisdom, let him ask of God, who gives generously to all without reproach, and it will be given him. But let him ask in faith, with no doubting, for the one who doubts is like a wave of the sea that is driven and tossed with the wind. For that person must not suppose that he shall receive anything from the Lord." Then, James adds the final punch: "he is a double-minded man, unstable in all his ways" (James 1:8).

God gives to all people liberally. Why? Because He owns it all and that's His nature. You could email me and ask me for a Maserati, but if I don't have one, you would be asking in vain. I can't give what I don't have. Conversely, God owns everything! He gives because He has. He doesn't care about flying first class, but when I asked, He miraculously allowed me to when He sent Kuran to give me his first-class upgrade (chapter 4, "Fear Sucks").

So what are the types of prayer? Are some more appropriate than others? I have no rule about this, just observation and personal experience. When we pray for ourselves, those are *requests* we are making to God. When we pray for others those are *supplications*. When we personally worship God, those are *praise* prayers to

Him. There are times for that (to be sure). There are also *deliverance* prayers, which are usually a subset of supplication, but we can pray for our own deliverance too. Let's take a deeper dive on deliverance.

Deliverance prayers are also known as *warfare prayers* because we are directing the focus of the prayer with the goal of targeting and defeating the devil in some way because he is vexing a person, group, or family with various temptations and habits: addiction, pride, lust, greed, the occult, and much more.

We never pray to satan or his emissaries; we pray only to God. However, once we affirm our position in God through prayer, we move on to the vital step of speaking to the demon(s). Let me repeat, *we don't pray to demons*, but we are empowered (and equipped) to speak to them out loud. Jesus did. We should.

The evil spiritual realm has one limitation (for sure), and that is that the devil cannot read our mind. He can toss bad thoughts into our mind but does not have unfettered access to it. It's like I call you on my cellphone, and after you answer, I say nothing, but I am thinking: *Hi, this is Mike Moore.* You don't receive my thoughts and say, "Hello, is anybody there?" before you hang up. Aside from phone texting, humans need to hear us speak. Same with the spiritual realm. If we don't speak, they don't hear.

The main effect of speaking to the devil and company is to remind them how defeated they are by the shed blood of Christ. Did you ever stop to think that our victory in Jesus comes at the expense of whatever (or whoever) was defeated? What was defeated was the power satan had over this world. Towards the end of God's Word, 1 John 3:8 says "Whoever makes a practice of sinning is of the devil, for the devil has been sinning from the beginning. The reason the Son of God appeared was to destroy the works of the devil."

What are "the works of the devil"? That would be everything he does to ruin our lives, kingdoms, governments, and so on. All evil has satan's fingerprints on it. At a minimum, he wants us to offend the Ten Commandments by:

1) idolatry,
2) worshiping created things (images),
3) using God's name as a byword or loosely,
4) ignoring the Sabbath,
5) dishonoring our parent(s),
6) killing,
7) adultery,
8) stealing from others,
9) lying, and
10) desiring things other people have.

This is a good start on satan's bucket list. We get into trouble when we adopt *any portion* of his bucket list into our lives.

Is there a model prayer? Like a silver-bullet prayer that ensures we get whatever we ask? No, but Jesus made a point to tell His disciples to pray "in this way,"

> Our Father, in Heaven,
> Glory and honor be to Your name.
> Your kingdom come,
> Your will be done,
> in Earth as it is in Heaven.
> Give us, today, our daily bread,
> and forgive our wrongdoings as we forgive the wrongdoing of others.
> And lead us away from temptation, and deliver us from evil.
> For Yours is the kingdom, the power, and the glory,
> Forever and ever, Amen!
> [paraphrase of Matthew 6:9–13]

That may not be how you memorized it as a youth, but that is what it says. On the whole, by praying this prayer we speak adoration, petition, confession, more petitions, and praise. It's not a law to pray that way. In fact, a one-sentence sincere prayer will arrest more of

God's attention than rattling off the Lord's Prayer mindlessly (by rote).

We can add to this what the apostle Paul taught the Philippian believers: "Do not be anxious about anything, but in everything by prayer and supplication with thanksgiving let your requests be made known to God. And the peace of God, which surpasses all understanding, will guard your hearts and your minds in Christ Jesus" (Philippians 4:6–7).

Note to self: Thank God when I pray.

I DARE YOU to divorce from a prayerless life. Make prayer an intentional priority. Any (past or present) godly man or woman you can name had an intentional, consistent time of prayer each day and other prayers, as needed, throughout the day.

> *You can do more than pray after you've prayed, but you cannot do more than pray before you have prayed. Pray often, for prayer is a shield to the soul, a sacrifice to God, and a scourge to [s]atan.*
> **– John Bunyan**
>
> *But when you pray, go into your room and shut the door and pray to your Father who is in secret. And your Father who*

sees in secret will reward you. And when you pray, do not heap up empty phrases as the Gentiles do, for they think that they will be heard for their many words. Do not be like them, for you Father knows what you need before you ask him.
– Matthew 6:6–8

May you always remember that effective prayer travels at the speed of faith.

26

BETTER RICH THAN BITCH

LET'S TALK ABOUT RICHES. Do you consider yourself rich?

Well, rich in what, Mike? Rich in money?

Maybe.

Rich in gold?

Maybe.

Rich in happiness? Rich in security? Rich in joy? Rich in peace? Rich in health? Rich in wisdom? Rich in intellect? Rich in compassion? Rich in forgiveness? Let's take a deep dive into what the Word says about riches. Right off, we see there are two kinds of riches: godly riches (that last for eternity) and worldly riches (that are temporary/fleeting). Now just because they are temporary doesn't mean they don't serve a purpose. That purpose is driven by our worldview, attitudes, and where we are with God.

Being wealthy is like being a beekeeper. The bees

represent your riches. If you treat the bees right, they provide honey for you and others who need it. If you don't treat the bees right, they either swarm away (to a better beekeeper) or you get stung.

The richest man who ever lived wrote these words: "There is a grievous evil that I have seen under the sun: riches were kept by their owner to his hurt" (Ecclesiastes 5:13). In other words, he never gave any away; he kept all for himself.

I don't know about you, but if Warren Buffett or Bill Gates or Elon Musk called my cellphone and said he wanted to tell me about his thoughts on riches, I would listen. Wouldn't you? Solomon, in his day and adjusted for centuries of inflation, had more wealth than those guys put together! What was Solomon's key phrase? Kept, or hoarded, by the owner. *Wealth isn't about striving to get; it is the power to give.*

Immigrant millionaire Andrew Carnegie said: "The man who dies rich, dies disgraced." Why disgraced? Because such a person squandered the opportunity to share his wealth with those in need (while he could). Remember, rich is great when we give a decent percentage to others. Rich is not great when we hoard it for ourselves and don't have a charitable exit strategy when we die.

Our friend Solomon observed a wealthy man who didn't have a righteous succession plan for his wealth.

He saw this man as saying: *There is no good end to all my labors, nor do my riches satisfy me, so why do I withhold my soul of good?* Translation: *I'll use it to meet my own desires (whatever I want) without a care toward helping others.* What does God say to that man, to you and me? "Whoever is generous to the poor lends to the Lord, and he will repay him for his deed" (Proverbs 19:17).

Being wealthy is a gift from God. Should a person enjoy it? Yeah, *to the max* but not at the expense of good stewardship. God tells us money is not the root of all evil, but *the love of money* is the culprit. You don't have to be rich to love money. It affects all economic classes of people.

Scripture lays it all out for us: "Do not love the world or the things of the world. If anyone loves the world, the love of the Father is not in him. [BOOM! Can you feel that?] For all that is in the world—the desires of the flesh, and the desires of the eyes and pride of life—is not from the Father but is from the world. And the world is passing away along with its desires, but whoever does the will of God abides forever" (1 John 2:15–17).

There can be a money component to "the desires of the flesh" (people we want), certainly a money component to "the desires of the eyes" (things we want), and a money component to "pride of life" (how we want people to see us). That's why the **love** of money is the root of all evil.

But destitution (having no money) doesn't make anyone a saint. Loving money, as a form of idolatry, takes away from our loving God. It puts money first and God second.

In Luke 16:13, Jesus flat out says that: "No servant can serve two masters, for either he will hate the one and love the other, or he will be devoted to the one and despise the other. You cannot serve God and money." Yet God can use the money He's given you to bless others, whether you are a billionaire or living from unemployment check to unemployment check. Years ago, I had a friend named Dave. He wanted to financially help a poor working man he met at a farmer's market, but Dave had no power (money on him) to give to anybody. The old man told Dave that he was short on rent. Frustrated because his wallet was empty, Dave looked at his friend Randy (standing nearby), who pulled out his wallet and handed the man three one-hundred-dollar bills and told him, "Take this," and the (shocked) old man did. Randy added: "This is what Jesus told me to give you."

See? That's what I'm talking about! Using the resources God has given you to be His conduit of blessing to others. It was good for Randy to be carrying around three hundred dollars. Randy probably didn't know he would be giving it away that day. God had a plan for that money. He has a plan for yours too!

In a nutshell, we are given earthly riches to steward as God would have us to. In those moments, we become His channel of tangible blessings. Let's be clear: making money through work, investments, inheritance, and so on is a gift from God (according to Deuteronomy 8:18). James 2:15–16 (my paraphrase) makes it clear: *If we see a man or woman without needed clothing and desperate for a meal, and (self- righteously) tell them to go "be warmed and be filled" but have not provided the obviously needed things for his or her body, what good is that?* James is saying we need to show our faith by our doing good in the lives of others; to do to others as we would have them do to us (if we were in their situation or struggle).

The godly riches are described as a good name, loving favor (in Proverbs), His glory, mercy, goodness, forbearance, long suffering (in Romans), exceeding riches of His grace, the unsearchable riches in Christ (in Ephesians), and Christ in you, the hope of glory (in Colossians)! These are the riches you keep. The earthly riches are the ones you give away AND use to raise a family, pay bills, enjoy life, and so on.

Jesus tells us in Matthew 6:19–20: "Do not lay up for yourselves treasures on earth, where moth and rust destroy and where thieves break in and steal, but lay up for yourselves treasures in heaven, where neither moth nor rust destroys and where thieves do not break in and steal." Later, Jesus says: "For where your treasure is, there your heart will be also" (Matthew 6:21). Imagine a treasure chest in your bedroom, full of your most precious possessions. What would a thief find if he looked inside? Your reputation? Your stocks and bonds? Your family? Your hobbies? Your things?

Let's get down to brass tacks. Would he find your faith in God in there? Would he find your hope of eternal salvation? Would he find your peace? Would he find joy? If not, why not? Perhaps it's time to clean out your treasure chest and refill it with the things man calls insignificant but God calls precious. The I AM declares it over you.

Moses learned this when he asked God, *Who shall I say sent me to deliver the people?* God said, *Tell the children of Israel: I AM.* Jesus said the same thing in John 8:58: "Before Abraham was, I am." Afterwards, they wanted to stone Him. They wanted to kill Jesus. WHY? Because they understood He was saying that I AM the One who spoke to Moses in the burning bush, equating Himself with YHWH God.

Later, when Jesus was in the garden of Gethsemane, all these soldiers drew near to Him and asked, *Are you Jesus?* He replied, *I AM, and all in His presence fell down.* Why did they fall down? Because they were struck by the power of the Almighty. That's the power of being in the presence of I AM.

So as we read the Word to get to know Jesus, He reveals Himself. As we pay attention to the things around us, the riches of Christ become more obvious. He reveals His word when we worship and praise Him and humble ourselves under Him. We may say: *God, I didn't ask to be born. I didn't ask to have this color of hair, this color skin, my height; where I'd be born, or who my mom and dad would be. I had no vote in anything. I didn't ask to be here, and here I am. You just constantly move towards me in life. You put the sun, the moon, and the stars in the sky to show me Your order. You demonstrate Your goodness every day, and most of the time, I'm not even aware of it.*

Help me see Your fingerprints on the affairs of my life.

The psalmist King David said (in Psalm 19) the heavens reveal who made the universe. It's God. It's perfect order. You can't completely take apart a Rolex watch, put its 220 moving pieces in a washing machine, and expect it to be a Rolex again in three hours. It's impossible to come together unless there's someone behind it. God is that someone. He says, *I AM. I'm everything. In Me, you have it all. In Me, you have everything.*

In the first chapter of Ephesians and elsewhere, it shows believers what we have in Christ because God chose us (in Him).

In Him we're holy.
In Him, we're blameless.
In Him, we're sons and daughters.
In Him, we're the beloved.
In Him, we're redeemed.
In Him, we're forgiven.
In Him, we've obtained an inheritance.
All things are in Him.
In Him, we've been sealed with the Holy Spirit of promise because we've received the Holy Spirit.
In Him, we receive mercy.
In Him, is compassion.
In Him, is peace.
Everything pertaining to life and godliness is in Him.
The worlds were created through Him.

Whom are we dealing with that God the Son would step down and give us all this, all this stuff with a focus on us? He says, *I'm your peace.*

We may say, *I don't feel or have peace.*

Jesus would answer, *If I'm in you, since I AM peace, you have peace. Don't ask Me for something you already have. Believe you already have it. I've given it to you.*

Let's say I give you a gift, a Movado watch. As you are holding it in your hand, you look at me and say, *Wow, Mike, I was wondering if you would give me a watch.*

What should my response be? I would look at you and admonish, *Why are you asking for a watch? I already gave one to you.*

I know, but I want a watch.

I'd have to say, *I put it in your hand—it's yours. Stop asking me for what you already have!*

Maybe we would be more aware of what we have if we started to use or apply what God's given us.

One of the most ridiculous prayers is **Lord, I want patience, NOW!** If we continue saying: "I want patience, Lord; I want patience, Lord; give me patience," we won't get the response we'd hoped for. He says, *I can't do that. How do I answer that question when I've given you the Holy Spirit—who is patience, who is love, who is mercy? I can't give you what you already have. You have to believe you have it. You must believe I'm that good at providing you everything pertaining to life and godliness the day you confessed Me as your Savior and Lord. That's the day you walked into the fourteenth generation, the moment you confessed Me as your Savior and King. You did nothing to prove you would ever follow Me or obey Me. Nothing. Yet I took away all your sins: past, present, and future. I put my Holy Spir-*

it in you. I was all in. I'm 100 percent all in. I'm betting on My Spirit. I'm betting on what I'm able to do in your life over time. I'm betting on My faithfulness, Mike, not your faithfulness. I'm betting that putting My love and My Spirit in you will transform you from the inside out because of what I did. Remember, everything pertaining to life and godliness is all yours as of day one, the moment you confessed Me as your Savior and your Lord.

When we go to Jesus and ask the Lord to fill our soul, forgive us, and trust what Jesus did at the cross, we are as fully complete in God as Billy Graham was.

We are as complete as any human being walking on the planet (that knows the Word of God) and has walked with God for one hundred years! We are as full of God as we ever will be. The difference is understanding and revelation in our knowledge of the Holy One.

That's why God gives us the OK to ask for wisdom in James 1:5: "If any of you lacks wisdom, let him ask God, who gives generously to all without reproach, and it will be given him." Wisdom is not a fruit of the Spirit. Wisdom is understanding our divine right, as a believer, to experience the fruit of the Spirit (love, joy, peace, patience, kindness, goodness, faithfulness, gentleness, self-control) and to live that out. We tend to forget that—which leads to foolishness and worldliness—so we ask God for wisdom to be our default, our primary way of dealing with life, people, and things.

When we don't recognize the riches of Jesus in our lives, we tend to complain (bitch). We complain to our family, friends, hairdresser, co-workers, neighbors, ourselves . . . anybody who will listen. Murmuring and complaining are among the most offensive sins to God. Those, along with fear, faithlessness, and being obstinate, became the undoing of the Israelites God had Moses lead out of Egypt. Bitching about life denies the fact God uses His power in your life. It implies you're simply a victim of a cruel world. You are not; He is holding you in His hands. Consider the Beatitudes:

Feeling lowly? *Blessed are the poor in spirit.*

Grieving? *Blessed are those who mourn.*

Feel non-assertive? *Blessed are the meek.*

Lack purpose? *Blessed are those who hunger after righteousness.*

Feeling exploited? *Blessed are the merciful.*

Tempted by sin? *Blessed are the pure in heart.*

Want to take sides or get revenge?

Blessed are the peacemakers.

Mistreated for your faith? *Blessed are those persecuted for righteousness' sake.*

Do evil people cancel you? *Blessed are those who are reviled and falsely accused for their faith in Jesus.*

God tells us to rejoice and be super glad for these hard things because He uses these things for good.

I DARE YOU to divorce from living as though Jesus has not given us His riches, including everything that pertains to life and godliness. **I dare you** to stop murmuring, bitching, and complaining about life, people, and circumstances.

> *A rich man is nothing but a poor man with money.*
> **– W. C. Fields**

> *And my God will supply every need of yours according to His riches in glory in Christ Jesus.*
> **– Philippians 4:19**

May the eyes of your heart be enlightened in order that you know the hope to which He has called you and the riches the He is providing you.

27

CONFESSIONS OF A SEAT SAVER

THERE'S A REASON that airlines let travelers with small children preboard. However, not all of those travelers make it to the gate in time for that. On a recent flight my friends were on, a couple and their young child were the last ones walking down the aisle. The flight attendants tried to find them a row, but the flight was too full. Desperate, the attendants made the passengers around them aware of the need. Ultimately, my friends, a couple in their sixties, gave their row to the younger family and sat in another row that had just two seats left.

Now, I am the last person to lecture anyone on giving up airline seats, right? But I can appreciate that flying in commercial airlines can teach us spiritual lessons. Remember Kuran in "Fear Sucks," chapter 4? It's like he woke up (the morning I met him on the plane) and prayed: *God, show me whom You want me to bless today.* So God set him in my row, and he gave his aisle seat to me. Mission accomplished, right? No. The act of Kuran letting go of his aisle seat was a trial run. When he passed that test, God sent in the big gun—his first-class upgrade. When that was handed to him, Kuran must have said to God, *I see what you are up to, Lord. You want to see how much I am willing to bless this man. I will not disappoint you.* So, he offered me the upgrade at no charge. Whether or not Kuran really knew God, he was doing God's work.

God wants to use people who are willing to give up their seat. All through Scripture, we see people giving up their seat: who they are, what they have, or what they could have been.

Abram gave up his home to follow God wherever He led.

Moses gave up his Egyptian royal position to lead the slaves.

Queen Esther risked her majestic life to approach the king about a planned Hebrew massacre.

Mary (of Galilee) gave up her reputation and dignity to get pregnant as a single woman.

Saul (of Tarsus) gave up his rise to Hebrew prominence to be an apostle to the Gentiles.

Jesus gave up His glorious presence in Heaven to come to planet Earth.

When we keep our seats, we lose our usefulness to God. It's a tough but real exchange. *What is the DNA of our seats?* Everything that we hold dear: reputation, wealth, education, family, possessions, hobbies, awards, titles, and so on; in short, our sense of self-worth. If we are not willing to give up our seats, then we are not worthy to be named a disciple of Jesus. "Whoever loves father or mother more than me is not worthy of me, and whoever loves son or daughter more than me is not worthy of me" (Matthew 10:37).

The apostle Paul had a lot of seats, as referenced above, and this is what he said about his seats in the Philippians 3:7–8 (NKJV): "What things [seats] were gain to me I have counted loss for Christ. Yet indeed I also count all things loss for the excellence of the knowledge of Christ Jesus my Lord, for whom I have suffered the loss of all things, and count them as rubbish, that I may gain Christ."

On the topic of seats (and pride), Jesus gave us a warning in Luke 14:8–11: "'When you are invited by someone to a wedding feast, do not sit down in a place of honor, lest someone more distinguished than you be invited by him, and he who invited you both will come and say to you, "Give your place [seat] to this person," and then you will begin with shame to take the lowest place. But when you are invited, go and sit in the lowest place, so that when your host comes he may say to you, "Friend, move up higher." *Then you will be honored in the presence of all who sit at the table with you.* [The lesson:] "For everyone who exalts himself will be humbled, and he who humbles himself will be exalted.'" My personal takeaway: If I don't give up my seat, God can (should) take it away from me so I can be humbled and receive His grace.

What Jesus said was experienced by a friend of mine who flies Southwest Airlines. As a budget airline, it doesn't have assigned seating, so your ticket lets you line up to go in with the As, Bs, or Cs at the gate. As each group boards, it's first come, first served for whatever seats are not already taken. His ticket was like C32, meaning he was in the last group to board. Nonetheless, there were a few others behind him.

At that moment, he remembered the words of Jesus, "Take the lowest place," so he waited for all the passengers to scan their tickets and go down the walkway. Finally, he got his ticket scanned and followed them. Right as he was about to step into the aircraft, he heard footsteps coming down the ramp. Some people were late getting to the gate and were barely let through. My buddy stepped aside and let them board before him. Little did he know, but a Southwest flight attendant saw it all happen. My friend began his aimless quest for a suitable middle seat between two passengers. Having found an OK option, he started to put his carry-on in the overhead luggage compartment. Just then, that same stewardess came up to him and said, "Follow me." Because of his act of letting all others on before him, she escorted him to a seat near the wing exit. It had the most legroom that a Boeing's 737 had to offer, which was a blessing because he is over six feet tall! He committed to having the worst seat, but she gave him one of the best seats. As I said, the domestic and international airlines I fly have all assigned seating.

That wouldn't work (or should I say, "fly") with the carriers I use.

I DARE YOU to divorce from a (my) seat-focused attitude. I love the common expression in Mexico: "*Mi casa, tu casa,*" which means "My house is your house," or, in our case, "My seat is your seat." This isn't about communism or nihilism; it's about treating others—even strangers—as Jesus would!

> The first question which the Priest and the Levite asked was: "If I stop to help this man, what will happen to me?" Then the good Samaritan came by, and by the very nature of his concern reversed the ques-

tion: "If I do not stop to help this man, what will happen to him?"
— **Rev. Martin Luther King Jr.**

May you excel in seat-giving more than you excel in seat-saving.

28

WHERE'S WALDO?

PERHAPS YOU'VE READ the children's book series called *Where's Waldo?* The challenge is find Waldo amid thousands of other tiny characters, animals, nature, and such on each double-page spread. Somewhere in there is a man with a red- striped hat and black-rimmed glasses. Sometimes he's obvious; at other times you'd swear they forgot to add him into the page. What happens when we look at portions of our life and ask: *Where's Jesus?*

Where's Jesus in our homes?
Where's Jesus in our businesses?
Where's Jesus at school?
Where's Jesus in the workplace?
Where's Jesus on the jobsite?
Where's Jesus in your marriage?
Where's Jesus in your singleness?
Where's Jesus in raising children?

Where's Jesus in your teaching?
Where's Jesus in your being taught?

Sure, there are parts of our lives where Jesus is certainly front and center: our quiet times, prayer times, worship times, reading the Word. But if you put all those times on a pie chart, that would be a little wedge in most people's day. Maybe an hour or two.

Two hours is only one-twelfth of your day! That's why it's a sliver on the pie chart called "today."

I have a friend named Keith Wheeler. He's been all over the world—carrying a twelve-foot cross. When he was just getting started, he didn't know where to be a light for Jesus. Even though he had never been in a bar in his life, he decided to go to a bar to share his new-found faith. He left the cross outside but took his Bible inside. After some seemingly vain attempts to share Jesus with the men, he found himself with the alpha male of the patrons. That bruiser of a fella lifted Keith on top of the pool table and told him to preach to the whole crowd. So . . . he did! Even though he was a babe in Christ, the Holy Spirit did all the (rest of the) heavy lifting, and that resulted in bringing every soul to Jesus! In that moment (because he was available), God spoke His love to every man in the bar through a rookie Christian. Cool huh? But it gets better . . .

They started to sing every hymn they could remember (and a few pop songs that they just knew). Next, there was prayer! After that, they said, "Preach again!" Back on the pool table, Keith preached his guts out, and the fellas got their second swig of Living Water. They were anxious, willing listeners. (Does that describe the people in your church?) Finally, Alpha Al said, "Guys, we gotta take up a collection for our preacher-brother." Without hesitation (or obligation) the patrons started laying cash on the pool table. One guy said, "I need to run home, but I'll be right back!" He left, and when he returned some minutes later, he dumped a sports bag of cash on the table. Keith said it was the largest collection of money he had ever gotten (for many years).

Note this wasn't just a payoff. It was an impromptu commissioning. They said, "Preacher Brother, there are guys like us in every bar in town. We're sending you to them so you can tell them what you told us." That led to the foundation of Keith's walk with God: *find a bar, go in, and preach*. He went to biker bars, gay bars, redneck bars—wherever he wouldn't be kicked out (or kicked in the face). It's like my buddy and fellow author, David Devine, says: "Without Jesus, our lives are full of empty." When Keith walked into that first bar, those men were full of empty (and they knew it). They were hungry for something more, something real.

The Word of God in Philippians 2 says we are to work out our salvation with fear and trembling. That may mean we take inventory (every now and then) to find the places in our lives that are way too empty of Jesus. We look at, say, our education, and Jesus is as hard to find as Waldo on the page. Friends, if we can't see Him, He's not there. Even if you find a piece of Him, is He just present, or is He prominent, or is He pre-eminent? *Jesus deserves to be pre-eminent everywhere and in every place.*

The guys at the bar were empty till Keith brought Jesus in with him. We are empty till we bring Jesus in with us. Try out these introspective yes-or-no questions about parts of your world:

Is He there?

If yes, is He merely present?

If yes, is He prominent in that area of your life?

If yes, is He pre-eminent in that area of your life?

If Jesus isn't there, then we need to invite Him in. If He is only prominent, then we change our attitudes and make Him pre-eminent. Jesus is either above and held in greatest regard or below and disregarded at whatever level (of disregard) we assign Him that day: barely, slightly, somewhat, clearly, or totally. It is a fool's folly to try to fit Jesus into the this-es or thats of our life. No, that's not our lane. Our lane is to let Jesus engulf all we do with Him in mind and with His kingdom's message in our hearts.

I DARE YOU to divorce from thinking you can control or limit Jesus. You can't. You can only control how much you will put on His altar and ride the wave of His will for your life.

The Secret Place

My heart is like a house
One day I let the Savior in
There are many rooms
Where we would visit now and then

But then one day He saw that door
I knew the day had come too soon
I said, "Jesus, I'm not ready
For us to visit in that room

'Cuz that's a place in my heart
Where even I don't go
I have some things hidden there
I don't want no one to know"

But He handed me the key
With tears of love on His face

He said, "I want to make you clean
Let Me go in your secret place"

So I opened up the door
And as the two of us walked in
 I was so ashamed
His light revealed my hidden sin

But when I think about that room now
 I'm not afraid any more,
 'Cuz I know my hidden sin
No longer hides behind that door

That was a place in my heart
Where even I wouldn't go
I had some things hidden there
 I didn't want no one to know

But He handed me the key
With tears of love on His face
And He made me clean
I let Him in my secret place
Is there a place in your heart

Where even you won't go?

– The Booth Brothers

Have you not known? Have you not heard? The LORD *is the everlasting God, the Creator of the ends of the earth. He does not faint or grow weary; his understanding is unsearchable.*
– Isaiah 40:28

May you fill each compartment, each cubbyhole, of your life with Jesus and gain His perspective on where you're going with life and those around you. **May Jesus be pre-eminent** on every page in your book of life.

29

CAN I DIVORCE MY SPOUSE?

I HAVE BEEN IN YOUR SHOES and did, as I shared earlier, see my marriage legally dissolved. I made a lot of excuses to justify breaking a vow I made to my wife and to the Lord. The following are some excuses believers (and unbelievers) make to satisfy our flesh in this HUGE decision:

We are not compatible.
She or he cheated on me (or even had an affair).
She or he doesn't love me anymore. I don't love him or her anymore.
She or he hates me. I hate her or him.
She or he is a bad influence on our children.
She or he is not the woman or man I married.
She or he is bad with money.
She or he won't get a job.
She or he walked out on me (and our kids).

She or he is in prison.

I don't get along with his or her family.

Would you agree the excuses above cover a lot of opinions we can have towards our spouses? Some are fairly trite. Some are very serious. I could write a whole book just going over each excuse, and maybe some others. That is not my lane for this book. I did not even want to bring divorce up in the context of couples struggling.

Yet I have to acknowledge your troubled marriage may be the very reason you bought this book—to arm yourself with sound scriptural reasons to justify divorcing your spouse. That is neither my purpose nor my goal. I offer no counsel on that for two reasons: (1) I don't know your situation well enough (that would include hearing your spouse's side of the story) and (2) I consider myself unworthy of guiding you in the way of breaking your vow before the Lord. Most Christians would say that, because I broke my vow to Him, I have no right to address that topic—and I appreciate where they are coming from. It may be judgmental, but even a blind squirrel gets an acorn once in a while.

I do make one request of you: don't get divorced from your spouse until you have gotten divorced from all the things mentioned in the previous chapters. In fact . . .

I DARE YOU to divorce from: believing that leaving church means leaving God; your past and worst fears; greed; pride; judging others; feeling unforgiven; seeing only the vile in people; the habit of being used as satan's spiritual sex toy—and thinking you are a good person because you're not an axe murderer; the *Me, Myself, and I* savior-complex, counterfeit Christianity; putting off the need for a Savior; anything less than devoted puppy love for God; majoring on the minors; making mountains out of your various molehills; a self-focused life; not getting right with your neighbors; living as though you were not dead; holding limiting assumptions; giving yourself titles; ignoring when God's calling you; comparing yourself with others; looking down on women; trying to manage without prayer; bitching about life/people/circumstances; having a self-focused attitude; AND thinking you can control or limit Jesus.

Is there a silver bullet among those things we can divorce from? There's only one way to find out. Your victory may come from divorcing one or more of those things. God knows, and He sent this book your way so you would know too!

> "But I say to you that everyone who divorces his wife, except on the ground of sexual immorality, makes her commit

adultery, and whoever marries a divorced woman commits adultery."
– Matthew 5:32

May you find the spouse God has for you—even if that means staying with the one you have or getting back with the one you used to have.